Tenor Volume 3

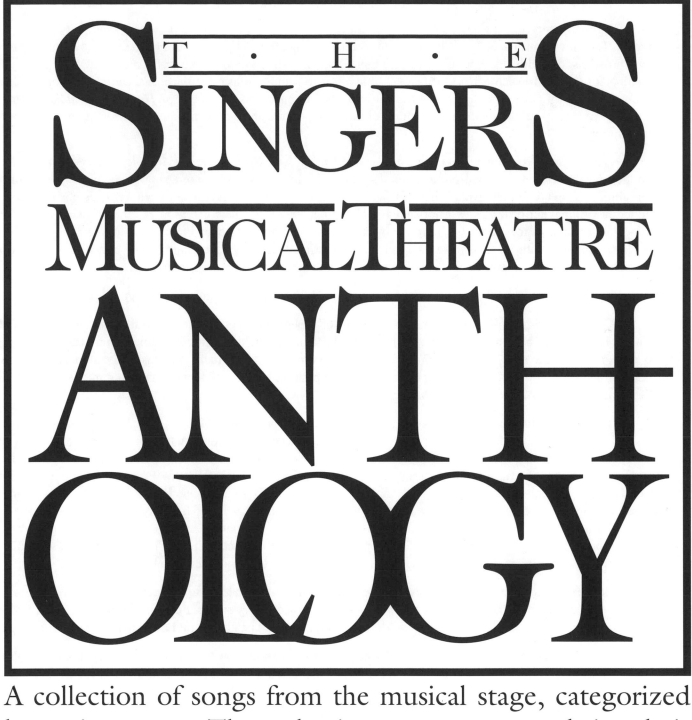

THE SINGERS MUSICAL THEATRE ANTHOLOGY

A collection of songs from the musical stage, categorized by voice type. The selections are presented in their authentic settings, excerpted from the original vocal scores.

Compiled and Edited by Richard Walters

Mark Carlstein and Milton Granger, Assistant Editors

ISBN 0-634-00976-1

HAL•LEONARD®
CORPORATION

7777 W. BLUEMOUND RD. P.O. BOX 13819 MILWAUKEE, WI 53213

Visit Hal Leonard Online at
www.halleonard.com

Foreword

The lively and ongoing interest in musical theatre may appear to be ironic in an age seemingly ruled by the media. The movie musical is dead (thank goodness for video and those classic movie channels!), show music is rarely ever broadcast on radio, and hoping to see any musical theatre on television—except for old movies—is usually like waiting for Godot. In such a world it takes a little effort to acquire a taste for musical theatre and a knowledge of shows, though to the devoted *conoscenti* it hardly feels like effort. As Volume 3 of *The Singer's Musical Theatre Anthology* proves, there is an amazing heritage of theatre repertoire and a growing appetite for it among singers of all descriptions.

As in the first two volumes for each voice type of *The Singer's Musical Theatre Anthology*, the editions of almost all the songs have been created from the piano/conductor score (or vocal score) of a show, allowing a more authentic rendition than standard piano/vocal sheet music. Original keys have been preserved whenever possible; occasionally either the original performing key is not known, or I chose to alter it for specific reasons. Common issues faced in creating solo editions of theatre music are removing chorus parts, eliminating other characters' lines, creating or deleting repeats, wrestling with musical form, and finding appropriate beginnings and endings. My aim is to present a performable excerpt from the show that stands alone musically, though is true to its context.

Categorizing musical theatre selections by conventional voice type remains a challenge.

For instance, where do you throw those "bari-tenor" songs that straddle those two ranges and could go either way? I have tried to be conservative in my criteria on this front. I quickly point out to singers and teachers that there is no exact science to this. In comparison, opera *fachs* are far more definite. In theatre music, it's not only about range, but also about vocal timbre and singing style. Many high baritones or versatile tenors have told me they use both the Tenor and Baritone/Bass volumes.

I included several numbers written for musical films rather than theatre. Most important, they are terrific songs. I also think they reflect a theatre sensibility, with an implied character in them. Fred Astaire had more great songs written for him than any other performer of the 20th century. Vocally he could be considered either a tenor or a lyric baritone, but I opted for tenor because of his light touch and ease in a higher tessitura. Thus, in this volume we have "Isn't It a Lovely Day," "Steppin' Out with My Baby," "and "I'm Putting All My Eggs in One Basket." "Easy to Love," sung by the surprisingly high tenor of Jimmy Stewart in the film *Born to Dance*, is included here, and an unusually dramatic song from a Disney film, "Go the Distance" from *Hercules* (with a show lyric more character-driven than the popular version of the song recorded by Michael Bolton). For Mandy Patinkin in the film *Dick Tracy*, Stephen Sondheim wrote "What Can You Lose?" I'm more than happy to have a chance to include it in a tenor theatre collection.

The theatre material included in this volume ranges from romantic leads to character songs, from the comic to the most dramatic, from the 1930s to 1998. Not every song is for every singer. I compile these collections with the needs of many different types of talent in mind. But everyone should be able to find more than a few terrific choices.

The twelve solo volumes of *The Singer's Musical Theatre Anthology* now total nearly 500 songs! The three volumes for any voice type offer a huge number of choices. The tenor books have 118 songs to choose from! Happy hunting.

Richard Walters, editor
August, 2000

THE SINGER'S MUSICAL THEATRE ANTHOLOGY
Tenor Volume 3

Contents

ABOUT THE SHOWS

The material in this section is by Stanley Green, Richard Walters, and Robert Viagas,
some of which was previously published elsewhere.

BORN TO DANCE
(film)

MUSIC AND LYRICS: Cole Porter
DIRECTOR: Roy Del Ruth
SCREENPLAY: Jack McGowan, B.G. DeSylva and Sid Silvers
CHOREOGRAPHER: David Gould
RELEASED: 1936, MGM

Although there had been film adaptations of his stage musicals, this was Cole Porter's first original screen score. It has a large cast of characters in a story that mixes sailors and show biz, culminating in the star of a show being replaced by an inexperienced young talent (Eleanor Powell), an all too obvious steal from the big Warner hit *42nd Street* of 1933. "Easy to Love" had been dropped from the score of the 1934 Broadway musical *Anything Goes*. After some rewriting it was heard in *Born to Dance*. James Stewart, in an early and uncharacteristic role, sings the song to Eleanor Powell in Central Park in the moonlight in his sweet, high tenor voice. (It's later reprised by Frances Langford.) The big finale of the movie, one of the most excessive numbers ever filmed, features Powell and a thousand chorus girls tapping away on a battleship.

BRIGADOON

MUSIC: Frederick Loewe
LYRICS AND BOOK: Alan Jay Lerner
DIRECTOR: Robert Lewis
CHOREOGRAPHER: Agnes de Mille
OPENED: 3/13/47, New York; a run of 581 performances

Two American tourists, Tommy Albright and Jeff Douglas, stumble upon a mist-shrouded Scottish town which, as they eventually discover, reawakens only one day every hundred years. Tommy, who enjoys wandering through the heather on the hill with a local lass, Fiona MacLaren, returns to New York after learning of the curse that has caused the town's excessively somnolent condition. True love, however, pulls him back to the highlands. The tale was made believable not only through its evocative score, but also through de Mille's emotion-charged ballets. During one of their sojourns, Tommy and Fiona find themselves swept up in a strange, sweet emotion that they agree is "Almost Like Being in Love."

CABARET

MUSIC: John Kander
LYRICS: Fred Ebb
BOOK: Joe Masteroff
DIRECTOR: Harold Prince
CHOREOGRAPHER: Ron Field
OPENED: 11/20/66, New York; a run of 1,165 performances

This moody musical captures the morally corrupt world of Berlin's demimonde just as the Nazis were coming to power. American writer Cliff Bradshaw moves in with Sally Bowles, the hedonistic star singer at a seedy nightclub. Soon, he comes to see all of Germany through the dark lens of that increasingly menacing cabaret, which is ruled over by a ghostly Emcee. Kander and Ebb cut "I Don't Care Much" from the original production, possibly because of its similarity to "So What," but restored it for the 1998 Broadway revival as a number for the Emcee to express the emotional numbness of his world. Contrast that with the anthem "Tomorrow Belongs to Me," whose soaring lyrics turned chilling when the audience realized that the young men singing it were Nazis.

CHICAGO

MUSIC: John Kander
LYRICS: Fred Ebb
BOOK: Fred Ebb and Bob Fosse
DIRECTOR-CHOREOGRAPHER: Bob Fosse
OPENED: 6/3/75, New York; a run of 872 performances

Based on Maureen Dallas Watkins' 1926 play *Roxie Hart*, this tough, flint-hearted musical tells the story of Roxie (Gwen Verdon), a married chorus girl who kills her faithless lover and almost manages to convince her geeky husband that it was all an innocent mistake. Roxie wins release from prison through the histrionic efforts of razzle-dazzle lawyer Billy Flynn (Jerry Orbach), and ends up as a vaudeville headliner with another "scintillating sinner," Velma Kelly (Chita Rivera). This scathing indictment of the American legal system, political system, media and morals may have been ahead of its time in its original 1975 production. It was also overshadowed by the opening of *A Chorus Line* the same season. But it came roaring back for a stylish, Tony-winning 1996 revival that has already run longer than the original. Roxie's husband Amos gets one solo, "Mister Cellophane," an emotional lament that all his life he's been the kind of man that people could look right through and pass right by. At the end, he even apologizes for taking up the audience's time.

DIAMONDS

MUSIC AND LYRICS: Various Writers

This was an Off-Broadway revue about baseball and included material from several writers. "What You'd Call a Dream," written by Craig Carnelia, has been most memorably sung by the songwriter himself.

DICK TRACY
(film)

MUSIC AND LYRICS: Stephen Sondheim (songs only; score by Danny Elfman)
SCREENPLAY: Jim Cash and Jack Epps Jr., based on the comic strip by Chester Gould
DIRECTOR: Warren Beatty
RELEASED: 1990

Dick Tracy is a colorful, highly stylish cinematic treatment of the classic comic strip. Dick is the heroic police detective fighting a sea of eccentric criminals. The film adds an interesting dimension to the character, as if Tracy is both repelled and fascinated by hoodlums. One of the recurring locations in the movie is a nightclub, which affords several prime opportunities for songs by Stephen Sondheim. The most famous of these is "Sooner or Later (I Always Get My Man)," sung by the vampy platinum blonde Breathless Mahoney (played by Madonna). "What Can You Lose" is sung in the empty nightclub by 88 Keys (Mandy Patinkin), joined by Breathless. It's a commentary on the yearning in the relationships among the film's principals, 88 Keys' unstated love for Breathless, her love for Tracy, Tess' love for Tracy. In the editor's opinion, the song ranks up at the top level of Sondheim's best work.

EASTER PARADE
(film)

MUSIC AND LYRICS: Irving Berlin
DIRECTOR: Charles Walters
SCREENPLAY: Sidney Sheldon, Frances Goodrich, Albert Hackett
CHOREOGRAPHER: Robert Alton (Fred Astaire, uncredited)
RELEASED: 1948, MGM

Yet another "songbag" picture, taking some proven Berlin hits, using a hit song as a title, adding a few new songs, two major movie stars, and whatever plot will hold it together. The picture was originally to have starred Gene Kelly opposite Judy Garland, but he withdrew from the production with a broken ankle. Fred Astaire, who had retired from the screen in 1946, was coaxed into taking Kelly's place and saving the production, and the result is the only teaming of Astaire and Garland. It's a nostalgic, theatrical story of vaudeville and Broadway in the year 1912. The movie is in the big-MGM-wholesome-holiday-family-picture tradition. "Steppin' Out with My Baby" is another in the large body of terrific songs written for Astaire, filmed with the chorus in the background at regular speed and the star in the foreground in graceful slow motion.

FOLLIES

MUSIC AND LYRICS: Stephen Sondheim
BOOK: James Goldman
DIRECTOR: Harold Prince
CHOREOGRAPHER: Michael Bennett
OPENED: 4/4/71, New York; a run of 522 performances

Taking place at a reunion of former Ziegfeld Follies-type showgirls, the musical deals with the reality of life as contrasted with the unreality of the theatre. *Follies* explores this theme through the lives of two couples, the upper-class, unhappy, Phyllis and Benjamin Stone, and the middle-class, also unhappy, Sally and Buddy Plummer. *Follies* also shows us these four as they were in their pre marital youth. The young actors appear as ghosts to haunt their elder selves. Because the show is about the past, and often in flashback, Sondheim styled his songs to evoke some of the theatre's great composers and lyricists of the past. A revised version of the show was presented in London in 1987, with some songs replaced with new numbers. "Make the Most of Your Music," Ben's song expressing the sunny philosophy of life he aspires to, comes from the London version. "Buddy's Blues" is an exercise in comic desperation, as he finds himself torn between his wife (whom he adores but who is indifferent to him) and his mistress (who worships him), whom he can't stand.

FOLLOW THE FLEET
(film)

MUSIC AND LYRICS: Irving Berlin
DIRECTOR: Mark Sandrich
SCREENPLAY: Dwight Taylor and Allan Scott
CHOREOGRAPHER: Hermes Pan (Fred Astaire, uncredited)
RELEASED: 1936, RKO Radio Pictures

Fred Astaire and Ginger Rogers had been first paired as supporting players in the 1933 musical *Flying Down to Rio*. In quick succession came *The Gay Divorcée, Roberta, Top Hat* and their fifth of nine RKO films together, *Follow the Fleet*. These movies are among the most entertaining and satisfying musical-comedy-fantasies ever made. *Follow the Fleet* is the most uncharacteristic of the pair's films. Rather than playing glamorous, wealthy, well-dressed characters in Art Deco settings, Ginger plays a gum-popping dance hall hostess and Fred, a common sailor. Rather than leaving the audience feeling short-changed, it gives us the duo in their most boisterous spirits. Typical of the rowdy, tap-dancing, good-time tunes is "I'm Putting All My Eggs in One Basket."

FOOTLOOSE

MUSIC: Tom Snow (additional songs by Eric Carmen, Sammy Hagar, Kenny Loggins and Jim Steinman)
LYRICS: Dean Pitchford
BOOK: Dean Pitchford and Walter Bobbie
DIRECTOR: Walter Bobbie
CHOREOGRAPHER: A.C. Ciulla
OPENED: 10/22/98, New York; still running as of 2/1/00

Based on the hit 1984 film musical of the same title, *Footloose* tells the story of a tiny midwest town where dancing is illegal. It seems the son of town preacher Rev. Shaw Moore was killed in a car accident after a dance some years back, and, in the aftermath, Rev. Moore moved the town council to enact the ban. Enter town newcomer Ren McCormack, who quickly becomes a rebel with a cause: he works to overturn the ban even as he courts Rev. Moore's pretty daughter Ariel. Despite mixed reviews, the show quickly became a favorite with younger audiences, partly because of its subject matter, and partly because of the pervasive high-energy dancing that broke the town's ordinances left and right. Ren has gotta dance! He expresses his compulsion in the restless "I Can't Stand Still." Comedy is supplied by his best friend in the new town, the goofy and likable Willard Hewitt. Willard isn't always sure what's the right thing to do, but always knows where to find out, as he explains in the country-style "Mama Says."

THE GONDOLIERS

MUSIC: Arthur Sullivan
LIBRETTO: W.S. Gilbert
OPENED: December 7, 1889, London

The Duke of Plaza-Toro arrives in Venice in desperate financial circumstances. He reveals to his daughter Casilda that she was wed to the son of the King of Barataria when the two were still infants. Furthermore, the boy in question must now assume the throne, since an uprising has killed his father. This is all good news to the Duke, but not to Casilda, for she and her father's drummer Luiz are in love. More bad news follows: The king in question is one of two gondoliers, Marco and Giuseppe, who were raised as brothers—but the woman who was their nursemaid must be obtained to determine which is which. As if this were't enough, both young men are newly married to a couple of nice Venetian girls. While all wait for the return of the nursemaid, Marco and Giuseppe go to Barataria to rule jointly. There they quickly miss their wives. Marco sings of the delights of female companionship ("Take a Pair of Sparkling Eyes"). By and by, everyone converges on Barataria—the young brides, the Duke and his retinue, and the nursemaid, who reveals that she had done some baby-swapping of her own, and that the real king is neither Marco nor Giuseppe, but the boy she raised as her son: Luiz! General rejoicing ensues, mixed with some regret as the two gondoliers leave their kingdom and return to the canals of Venice.

HERCULES
(film)

MUSIC AND LYRICS: Alan Menken and David Zippel
SCREENPLAY: Ron Clements, Donald McEnery, Bob Shaw and Irene Mecchi
DIRECTORS: John Musker and Ron Clements
RELEASED: 1997, Walt Disney

Hercules marked Disney's return to the lighter musical comedy of its earlier animated musicals. In this snappy romp through Greek mythology *Hercules* tells the story of the Greek hero, born of the gods but not quite immortal. As half man/half deity and all teenager he tries to fit in, but it's painfully obvious to everyone, including himself, that he doesn't and never will. He sets out to find his "place" in the world, at whatever cost ("Go the Distance"). Learning that he is the son of Zeus and must prove himself a "true hero" to regain his place among the deities, he enlists the help of a doting Pegasus and a satyr named Phil. He becomes a famous hero, battling monsters, Hades, the Titans, and even saving Mt. Olympus, but in the end it is his love for Meg and his self-sacrifice to save her which makes him a true hero. Having regained his birthright he then gives it up to remain on earth with her. "Go the Distance" earned an Oscar nomination for Menken and Zippel and was also a hit for Michael Bolton, who sang it (with adapted pop lyrics) during the end credits.

JACQUES BREL IS ALIVE AND WELL AND LIVING IN PARIS

MUSIC: Jacques Brel
LYRICS: Jacques Brel, others (in French); English lyrics by Eric Blau and Mort Shuman
OPENED: 1968, New York

A long running intimate Off-Broadway hit, the revue is a collection of some 25 songs by French songwriter Jacques Brel (he wrote both music and lyrics for some, lyrics only for others). The show is conceived for 4 players (2 men, 2 women), and the songs are full of contrasts in subject matter, from the draft, to old age, to bullfights, to death, to love. A film version was released in the early '70s.

JEKYLL & HYDE

MUSIC: Frank Wildhorn
LYRICS AND BOOK: Leslie Bricusse
DIRECTOR: Robin Phillips
CHOREOGRAPHER: Joey Pizzi
OPENED: 4/28/97, New York; still running as of 5/1/00

Based on Robert Louis Stevenson's 1886 novella *Dr. Jekyll and Mr. Hyde*, this show took nearly a decade to arrive on Broadway. However, the first full score by pop composer Frank Wildhorn was already familiar to most lovers of musical theatre from two widely circulated concept albums. These proved especially popular among professional skaters for the background music of their routines. A North American tour also helped make the show familiar to most of the rest of America before arriving in New York. As in the Stevenson book, a well-meaning scientist, Dr. Henry Jekyll, invents a potion that separates the noble side of man's nature from the evil, bestial side. Using himself as guinea pig, Jekyll soon finds he has unleashed an uncontrollable monster, Mr. Hyde, who cuts a murderous swath through London. The first time Hyde emerges from the midnight recesses of Jekyll's psyche, he exults in the power of his newly liberated menace, in "Alive!"

JOSEPH AND THE AMAZING TECHNICOLOR® DREAMCOAT

MUSIC: Andrew Lloyd Webber
LYRICS: Tim Rice
OPENED: Premiered 5/12/68, London; first revision 1973, London; Broadway debut: 11/18/81, a run of 824 performances

The musical lasted all of 15 minutes in its first form, written for a school production in 1968, the first produced collaboration by the young Lloyd Webber (who was 20 at the time) and Rice. By 1973 the piece had been expanded to about 90 minutes, and was staged in the West End. The first New York performance took place at the Brooklyn Academy of Music in 1976, and a Broadway run finally commenced in 1981. Somewhat of a forerunner to *Jesus Christ Superstar*, which is also based on Biblical sources, *Joseph* is told entirely in an eclectic mix of rock, country, vaudeville and calypso song styles. Drawn from the Old Testament, the musical tells the story of Joseph, Jacob's favorite of 12 sons, who is given a remarkable coat of many colors. His jealous brothers sell him into slavery, and he is taken to Egypt, where he interprets the dream of Pharaoh. His wise prophecy so impresses Pharaoh that Joseph is elevated in honor and position, and put in charge of saving the country from famine. At the joyous climax of the show, Joseph leads his reunited (and forgiven) family in an homage to optimism and faith, "Any Dream Will Do."

KISMET

MUSIC AND LYRICS: Robert Wright and George Forrest (Based on music by Alexander Borodin)
BOOK: Charles Lederer and Luther Davis
DIRECTOR: Albert Marre
CHOREOGRAPHER: Jack Cole
OPENED: 12/3/53, New York; a run of 583 performances

The story of *Kismet* was adapted form Edward Knoblock's play, first presented in New York in 1911 as a vehicle for Otis Skinner. The music of *Kismet* was adapted from themes by Alexander Borodin first heard in such works as the "Polovetzian Dances," ("He's In Love," "Stranger in Paradise") and in "Steppes of Central Asia," ("Sands of Time"). The action of the musical occurs within a twenty-four hour period, in and around ancient Baghdad. A Public Poet (Alfred Drake) assumes the identity of Hajj the beggar and gets into all sorts of Arabian Nights adventures. His schemes get him elevated to the position of emir of Baghdad and get his beautiful daughter Marsinah (Doretta Morrow) wed to the handsome young Caliph (Richard Kiley). The film version was made by MGM in 1955, with Howard Keel as Hajj. Vincente Minnelli directed. On the eve of his wedding, the Caliph calls for the finest of everything to be spread before his bride to celebrate the "Night of My Nights."

MARTIN GUERRE

MUSIC: Claude-Michel Schönberg
BOOK: Alain Boublil and Claude-Michel Schönberg
LYRICS: Alain Boublil and Stephen Clark
DIRECTOR: Conall Morrison
MUSICAL STAGING AND CHOREOGRAPHY: David Bolger
OPENED: June, 1996, London; a run of over 700 performances

There have been several major revisions of the Boublil/Schönberg musical since its inception in 1991. Besides the musical, the 16th century legend inspired the books *The Wife of Martin Guerre* by Janet Lewis, and *The Return of Martin Guerre* by Natalie Zemon Davis. The 1982 film *The Return of Martin Guerre*, starring Gerard Depardieu, is based on the Davis novel. In 1560 the French Catholic mercenary Martin Guerre tells his friend, Arnaud du Thil, of his childhood in the village of Artigat, and of his arranged marriage to Bertrande du Rols. The villainous Guillaume, rebuffed by Bertrande, had convinced the superstitious villagers that Martin's failure to conceive an heir brought on their crop failures. Martin was exiled, later to join the mercenary corps ("I'm Martin Guerre"). Martin is stabbed while saving Arnaud's life. Arnaud escapes and goes to Artigat, where he is mysteriously believed to be Martin Guerre returning after seven years. Bertrande falls in love with Arnaud, even though she knows he is not Martin. Guillaume, still hoping for Bertrande, charges Arnaud with fraud for impersonating Martin Guerre. At a dramatic moment the real Martin Guerre returns and denounces Arnaud. Learning of the true love between Bertrande and Arnaud, in the spirit of friendship Martin decides to let them go. Protecting Martin from Guillaume's knife, Arnaud is stabbed and dies.

THE PAJAMA GAME

MUSIC: Richard Adler
LYRICS: Jerry Ross
BOOK: George Abbott and Richard Bissell
DIRECTORS: George Abbott and Jerome Robbins
CHOREOGRAPHER: Bob Fosse
OPENED: 5/13/54, New York; a run of 1,063 performances

When Frank Loesser was approached to write the score of a musical adaptation of Richard Bissell's novel *7 1/2 Cents*, he had to turn it down. But he did recommend a young team, Richard Adler and Jerry Ross, who had never before written songs for a book musical. They quickly went to work with Bissell, another Broadway newcomer, in collaboration with veteran director George Abbott. (Other neophytes involved were co-director Jerome Robbins, choreographer Bob Fosse, and the trio of producers.) *The Pajama Game* follows the hijinks at the Sleep-Tite Pajama Factory in Cedar Rapids, Iowa, where Sid Sorokin, the new plant superintendent, has taken a shine to Babe Williams, a union activist. Their romance suffers a setback when the workers go on strike for a seven-and-a-half cents hourly raise. But eventually management and labor are again singing in harmony. Stars John Raitt and Eddie Foy, Jr. repeated their roles in the 1957 movie version, which also starred Doris Day. The show was revived on Broadway in 1973 with Hal Linden, Babara McNair and Cab Calloway. The show produced several standards, most notably "Hey There," in which Sid warns himself against falling in love.

PARADE

MUSIC AND LYRICS: Jason Robert Brown
BOOK: Alfred Uhry
DIRECTOR: Harold Prince
CHOREOGRAPHER: Patricia Birch
OPENED: 12/17/98, New York; a run of 84 performances

The musical that opened at New York's Lincoln Center got mostly negative reviews for its relentlessly downbeat subject matter: the true story of Leo Frank, a Jewish factory manager accused of—and lynched for—the murder of Mary Phagan, an underage female worker, in 1913 Atlanta. But the sterling cast album released a few months later helped build a cult of devoted fans for this short-run musical, which went on to win the 1999 Tony Awards for Best Score and Best Book of a Musical. The song's opening number, "The Old Red Hills of Home," sets the scene, as a young Confederate soldier heads off to war for the land he loves, and later, as a one-legged veteran, bitterly looks back on what was lost. In Act II, with Leo under a death sentence, his faithful wife Lucille discovers a piece of evidence that could exculpate him. Wild with joy, Leo sings of his new lease on life—and his debt to Lucille—in "This Is Not Over Yet."

PIPPIN

MUSIC AND LYRICS: Stephen Schwartz
BOOK: Roger O. Hirson
DIRECTOR-CHOREOGRAPHER: Bob Fosse
OPENED: 10/23/72, New York; a run of 1,944 performances

Stephen Schwartz collaborated on the original version of *Pippin*—then titled *Pippin Pippin*—when he was still a student at Carnegie Tech. But it was not until the success of *Godspell* and his collaboration with Leonard Bernstein on *Mass* that a producer was willing to take a chance on him or his work. As insurance, Stuart Ostrow brought in playwright Roger O. Hirson to rewrite the book and, most significantly, Bob Fosse to serve as director-choreographer (and, eventually, uncredited co-librettist). Like many young people in the early 1970s, Pippin, son of the medieval emperor Charlemagne, experiments with a series of different lifestyles, seeking glory first in war, then as a lover, and finally as a leader of social causes. Failing at all three, he is happy to compromise by settling down to middle-class domesticity with a pretty and understanding widow. Fosse took this little parable and put his conceptual stamp on it by expanding it into a razzle-dazzle magic show within the framework of a commedia dell'arte performance. Helping to give the production a unifying concept was another Fosse touch, a half-God, half-Devil "Leading Player," a character developed from the Emcee in *Cabaret*. The audience is introduced to Pippin with a song in which he claims a special "Corner of the Sky" as his birthright.

THE PIRATES OF PENZANCE

MUSIC: Arthur Sullivan
LIBRETTO: W.S. Gilbert
OPENED: December 31, 1879, New York

The only one of Gilbert and Sullivan's works to have its official premiere outside London, it did in fact receive one prior performance in England for purposes of copyright registration. Twenty-one-year-old Frederic, bound by his sense of duty to serve out his apprenticeship to a band of pirates, has reached the end of his indentures and decides henceforth to oppose the cutthroat crew rather than join them. After leaving the pirates, Frederic happens upon a party of young women and appeals to them for pity ("Oh, Is There Not One Maiden Breast"). The pirates then arrive on the scene, determined to marry the young ladies, but the girls' father, Major-General Stanley, enters just in time and wins clemency by claiming to be an orphan. Frederic, at first duty-bound to destroy his former comrades, rejoins them when he finds that his apprenticeship extends to his twenty-first birthday, and, having been born on February 29, he has so far had only five birthdays. But in the end, the pirates yield to the police at the invocation of Queen Victoria's name, and when it is revealed that they are actually wayward noblemen, they earn their pardon and permission to marry the Major-General's daughters.

RENT

MUSIC, LYRICS AND BOOK: Jonathan Larson
DIRECTOR: Michael Greif
CHOREOGRAPHER: Marls Yearby
OPENED: 2/29/96, New York; still running as of 2/01/00

One of the emblematic Broadway shows of the 1990s, Jonathan Larson's alternative-rock musical relocates the story of opera's *La Boheme* to the '90s in New York's Bohemian East Village. Instead of dying of consumption, the central character, also named Mimi, is dying of AIDS. The characters are a mix of various types of contemporary artists: a filmmaker, an HIV-positive musician, a drug-addicted dancer, a drag queen. Despite struggles, the friends remain devoted to one another. The compelling alternate-rock score has a gritty realism that had special appeal for young theatregoers. A parable of hope, love and loyalty, *Rent* received great acclaim, winning the Pulitzer Prize for Drama, a Tony Award for Best Musical, and many other awards. It quickly transferred from Off-Broadway's New York Theatre Workshop to a Broadway theatre that was redesigned especially for the show, to capture its East Village atmosphere. Bound up with the show's message of the preciousness of life is the tragic real-life story of its composer/librettist Jonathan Larson, who died suddenly the night of the final dress rehearsal before the first Off-Broadway performance. In "One Song Glory," the musician, Roger, sings of his dream of writing one great song. Near the end of the show, as Roger holds a dying Mimi in his arms, he tries to tell her what he really feels for her, in "Your Eyes."

70, GIRLS, 70

MUSIC: John Kander
LYRICS: Fred Ebb
BOOK: Fred Ebb and Norman L. Martin
DIRECTORS: Paul Aaron and Stanley Prager
CHOREOGRAPHER: Onna White
OPENED: 4/15/71, New York; a run of 36 performances

After the dark subject matter of their *Cabaret* and *Zorba*, Kander and Ebb chose a farcical story for their 1971 musical: A group of aging but spry New Yorkers plot a big robbery to save the residence hotel where they live. The musical was structured as a series of vaudeville turns to show off the talents of the original stars, who included Hans Conreid and Mildred Natwick. The oldsters blow a heartfelt raspberry in "Coffee in a Cardboard Cup," which they see as a symbol of everything that's wrong with modern life.

SUNSET BOULEVARD

MUSIC: Andrew Lloyd Webber
LYRICS AND BOOK: Don Black and Christopher Hampton
DIRECTOR: Trevor Nunn
CHOREOGRAPHER: Bob Avian
OPENED: 11/17/94, New York; a run of 977 performances

Sunset Boulevard, based on the 1950 Billy Wilder film, provided Broadway and the West End with one of the greatest diva vehicles ever. Dealing with a tortured woman whose advancing age leads to rejection and madness, this musical shows the debilitating aftereffects of Hollywood stardom in all their gothic glory. The show premiered in London in 1993 with Patti LuPone as the former silent screen star Norma Desmond who is desperate to make a comeback (though she loathes that word). After several lawsuits, the Broadway role went to Glenn Close, who had played the show in Los Angeles. The story involves young screenwriter Joe Gillis who stumbles into Norma Desmond's life. She falls in love with him, and he accepts her lavish attention. Miss Desmond has a pathetic plan to return to the screen with her own hopelessly overwritten adaptation of Salome. She thrills when the studio invites her to come by. But she's then crushed when she learns they don't want her—they want her vintage car, as an antique prop. Her life and sanity quickly fly apart, with tragic consequences for all. In a solo addressed directly to the audience, Joe tries to explain his decision to embrace all the phoniness and rotted dreams of Hollywood in the show's lurching title song.

TITANIC

MUSIC AND LYRICS: Maury Yeston
BOOK: Peter Stone
DIRECTOR: Richard Jones
CHOREOGRAPHER: Lynne Taylor-Corbett
OPENED: 4/23/97, New York; a run of 804 performances

The whole idea of a musical about the sinking of the luxury liner *Titanic* was unsettling to many Broadwayites. Few thought Yeston, Stone and company could pull it off. And reports of technological glitches during the early previews threatened to turn the whole project into a joke. And yet, when they finished counting the Tony ballots in 1997, *Titanic* won for Best Musical. Credit the strength of Yeston's score that explored the emotional nuances of a whole tapestry of characters and situations. The music takes theatregoers inside the head of the captain, the shipbuilder, the millionaires, the social climbers and the illiterate immigrants, each with their dreams and worries that are changed forever by the events of that fateful journey. In "Barrett's Song," a man who shovels coal into the mighty ship's boilers wonders how a simple country lad like himself has come to be in such a hellish place, and worries that perhaps he knows more about safety than the men on the bridge. Discovering the magic of the newly-invented wireless radio, Barrett uses it to propose to his sweetheart Darlene, bittersweetly promising in this Irish air ("The Proposal") that he'll be in her arms soon. A sense of foreboding also fills the edgy waltz "No Moon," sung by the lookout who's supposed to be watching for icebergs, but who cannot see a thing in the impenetrable darkness.

TOP HAT
(film)

MUSIC AND LYRICS: Irving Berlin
DIRECTOR: Mark Sandrich
SCREENPLAY: Dwight Taylor and Allan Scott
CHOREOGRAPHER: Hermes Pan (Fred Astaire, uncredited)
RELEASED: 1935, RKO Radio Pictures

This is the movie that forever clinched the image of Fred Astaire in a top hat and tuxedo. It's the fourth movie starring Astaire and Ginger Rogers (preceded by *Flying Down to Rio*, *The Gay Divorcée* and *Roberta*). *Top Hat* follows the same look and characters established in *The Gay Divorcé*e—sophisticated, light in tone, well dressed characters, an irreverent script, romantic sparks, all in smart Art Deco. The movie contains the classic Astaire-Rogers number "Cheek to Cheek." On the lighter side is Astaire's "Isn't This a Lovely Day (To Be Caught in the Rain?)." Movie musicals of the '30s don't get any better than this one.

WHEN PIGS FLY

MUSIC: Dick Gallagher
SKETCHES AND LYRICS: Mark Waldrop
CONCEIVED BY: Howard Crabtree and Mark Waldrop
OPENED: 8/14/96, New York; a run of 840 performances

As in his previous campy, satirical musical comedy revue *Whoop Dee Doo!*, writer/designer Howard Crabtree takes an incident from his past and pumps it full of laughing gas. Central character "Howard," who not coincidentally resembles Crabtree, is trying to put together a satirical, gay-themed revue, not unlike the one we're watching. Naturally, everything goes wrong. The title refers to a cutting comment made by young Crabtree's guidance counselor, that he'd be working on Broadway "when pigs fly." The counselor's spirit appears in the show, persistently belittling Howard's determination to get the show on its feet. Sadly, Crabtree died just days before the opening of this Off-Broadway hit. "Quasimodo" is the show's send-up of community theatre attempts to musicalize unmusical subjects, in this case *The Hunchback of Notre Dame*. It also parodies the Disney musical. The song includes the ineffable line, "I've got a hunch—I'm in love!"

WORKING

MUSIC AND LYRICS: Stephen Schwartz, Craig Carnelia, James Taylor, Micki Grant,
Mary Rodgers and Susan Birkenhead
BOOK AND DIRECTION: Stephen Schwartz
CHOREOGRAPHER: Onna White
OPENED: 5/14/78, New York; a run of 25 performances

Adapted from Studs Terkel's Pulitzer-winning book of interviews with all walks of working men and women, this revue-type musical followed a typical work day around the clock. We meet a waitress, a fireman, a builder, a teacher, a retiree, a cleaning lady, a parking lot attendant, a millworker, and many more, offering a cross-section of attitudes about the kind of work people do and why they do it. Some of their stories are funny, some stoic, some deeply touching. As Terkel put it, "Its theme is about a search for daily meaning as well as daily bread, for recognition as well as cash." To express its eclectic characters, *Working* had a score made up of songs by an assortment of writers with a variety of distinctive styles and ethnic backgrounds. In the wake of *A Chorus Line*, the doors seemed open for this group-character type of show. But its quick failure was devastating to Schwartz, who had already written three of the longest-running musicals of the 1970s, *Pippin*, *Godspell* and *The Magic Show*. On April 14, 1982, a TV version of *Working* aired on PBS. In "The Mason," a bricklayer looks up at the edifice he helped erect, and sees a monument to himself.

ALMOST LIKE BEING IN LOVE

from *Brigadoon*

Words by ALAN JAY LERNER
Music by FREDERICK LOEWE

Andante

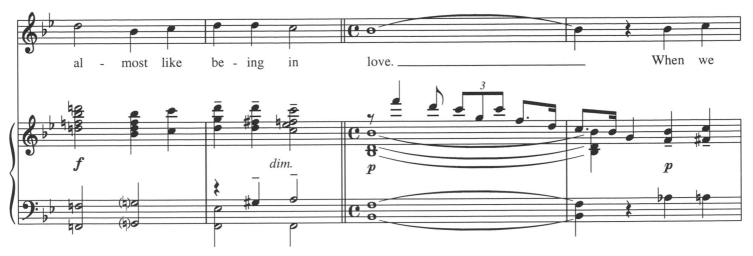

al - most like be - ing in love. _____ When we

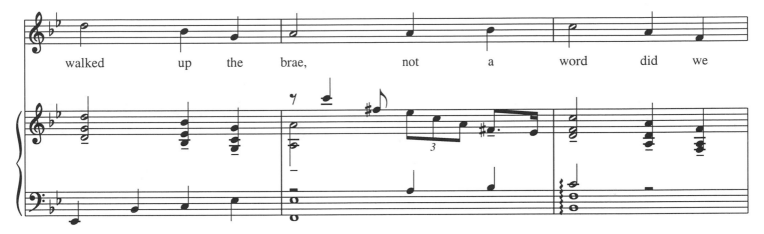

walked up the brae, not a word did we

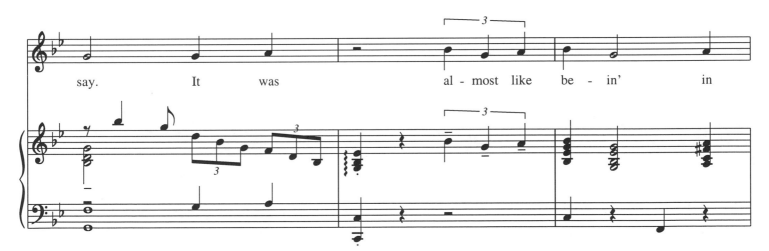

say. It was al - most like be - in' in

love. _____ But your arm link'd in

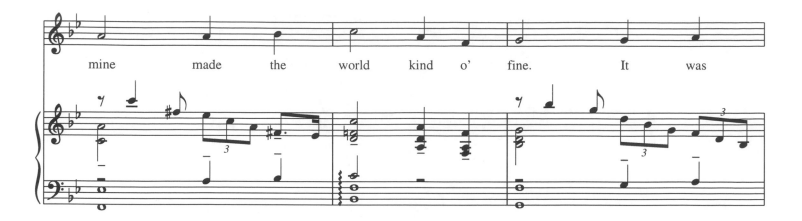

mine made the world kind o' fine. It was

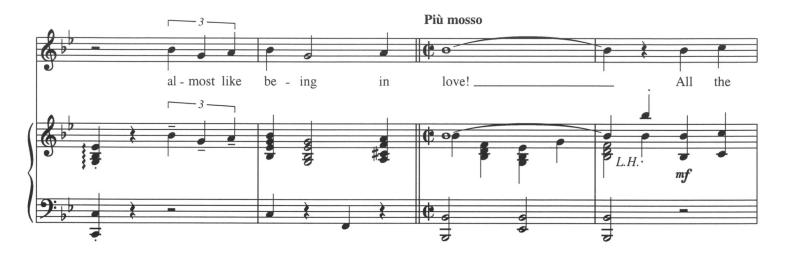

al - most like be - ing in love! _____ All the

Più mosso

Tempo I

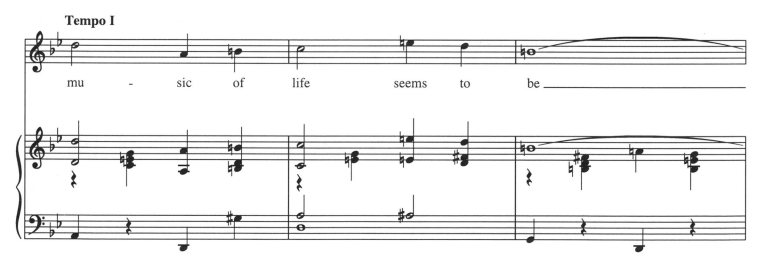

mu - sic of life seems to be _____

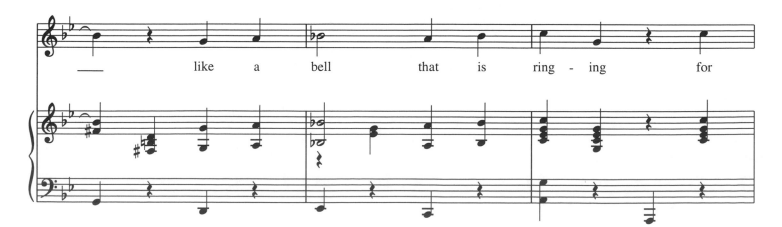

____ like a bell that is ring - ing for

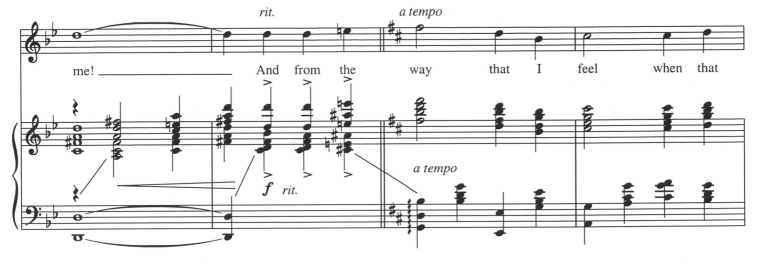

rit.   *a tempo*

me! _____ And from the way that I feel when that

bell starts to peal, I would swear I was fall - in', I could

swear I was fall - ing, It's al - most like

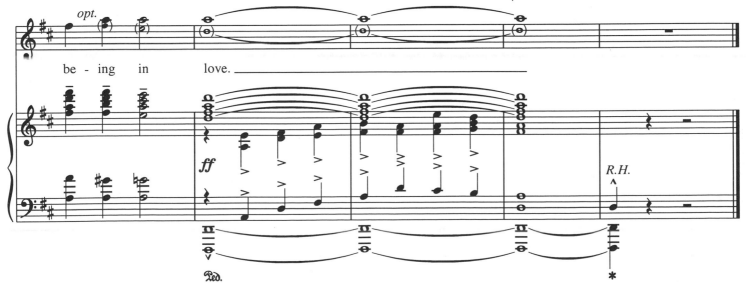

be - ing in love. _____

EASY TO LOVE
(You'd Be So Easy to Love)
from *Born to Dance*

Words and Music by
COLE PORTER

keep ev - 'ry home-fire burn - ing for, _____ We'd be so

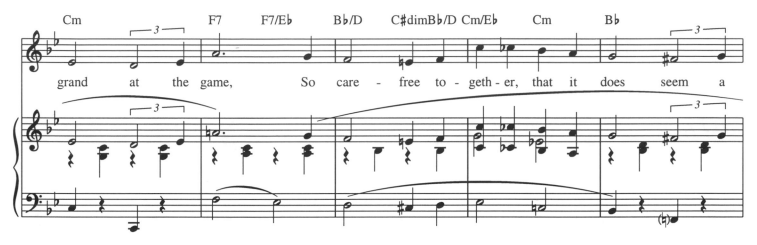

grand at the game, So care - free to - geth - er, that it does seem a

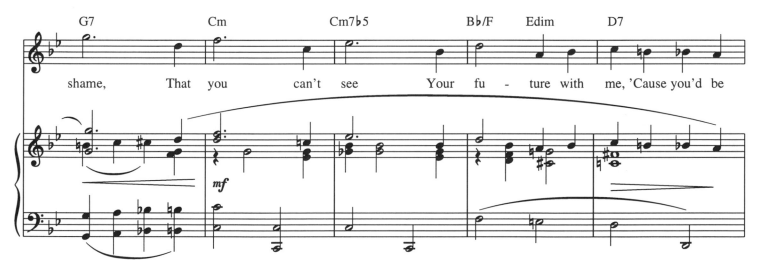

shame, That you can't see Your fu - ture with me, 'Cause you'd be

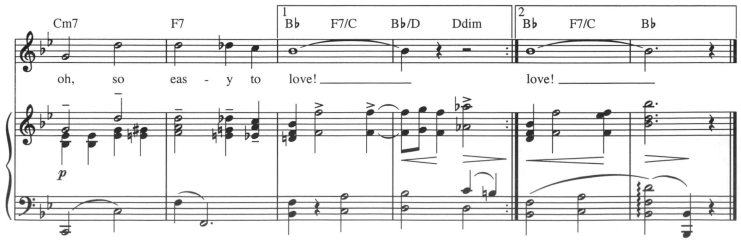

oh, so eas - y to love! _____ love! _____

TOMORROW BELONGS TO ME

from the musical *Cabaret*

Words by FRDD EBB
Music by JOHN KANDER

*The tenor soloist sings with a male chorus in the show.

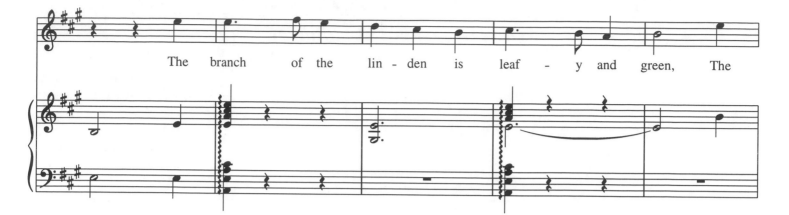

The branch of the lin - den is leaf - y and green, The

Rhine gives its gold to the sea. _____ But some - where a

glo - ry a - waits un - seen, To - mor - row be - longs to

me. _____ Oh, fa - ther-land, fa - ther - land

show us the sign your chil - dren have wait - ed to

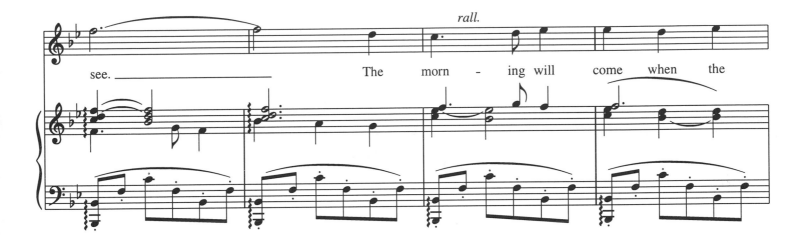

see. _____ The morn - ing will come when the

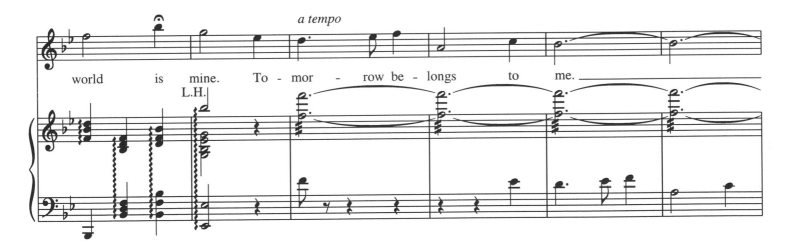

world is mine. To - mor - row be - longs to me. _____

To - mor - row be - longs to me.

I DON'T CARE MUCH
from the musical *Cabaret*

Words by FRED EBB
Music by JOHN KANDER

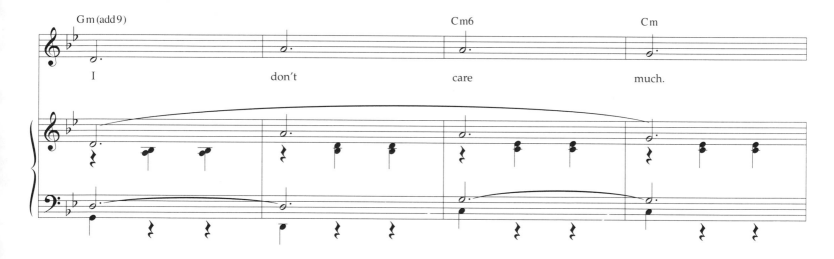

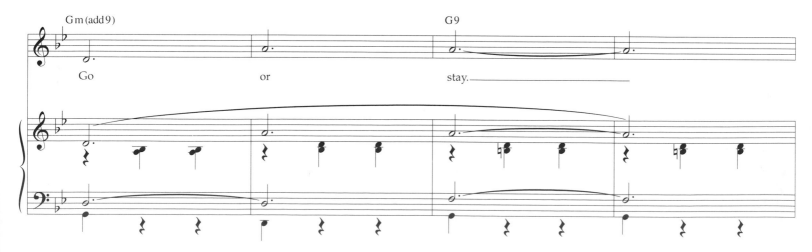

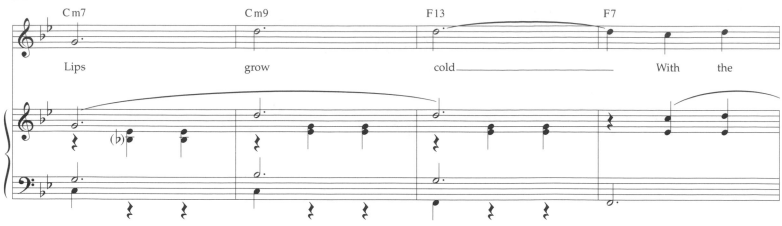

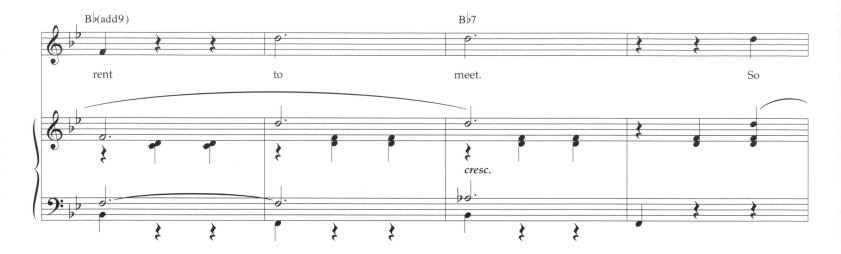

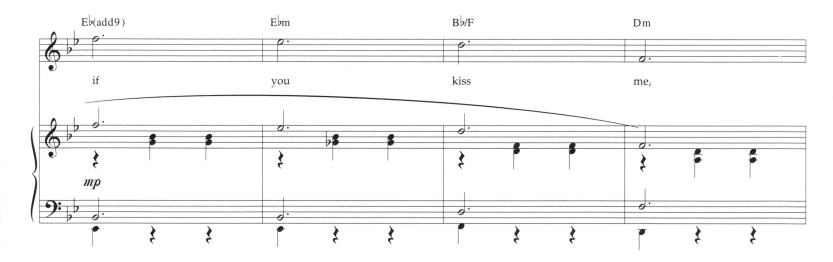

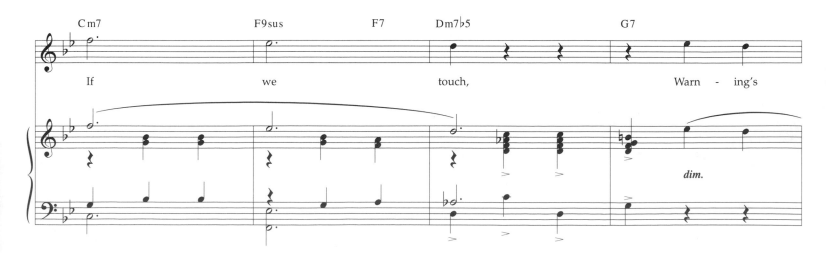

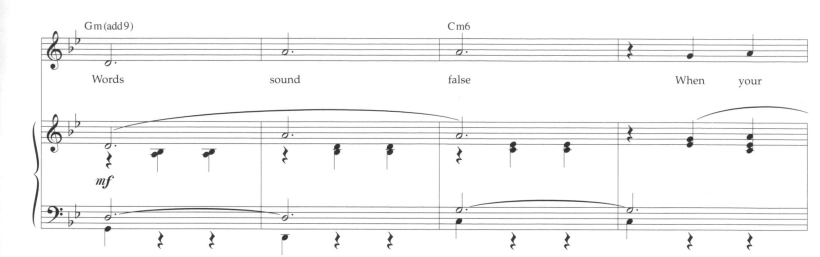

Words   sound   false   When your

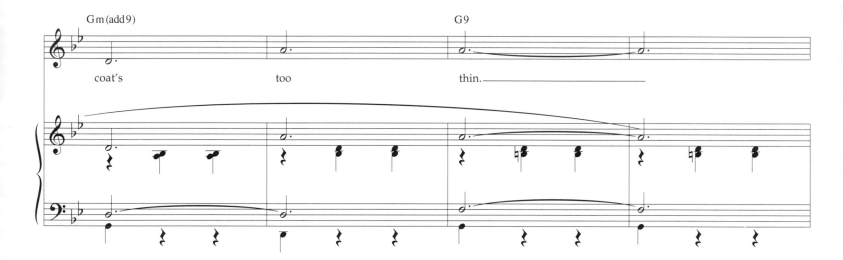

coat's   too   thin.

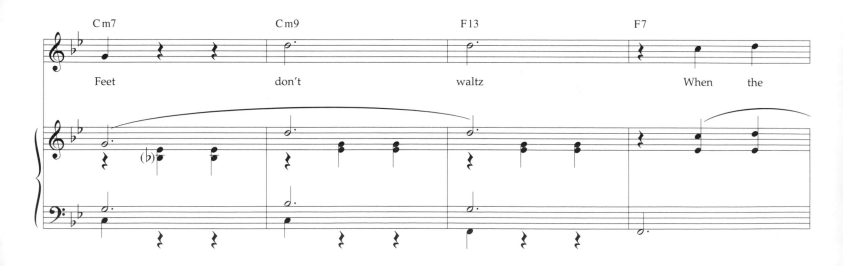

Feet   don't   waltz   When the

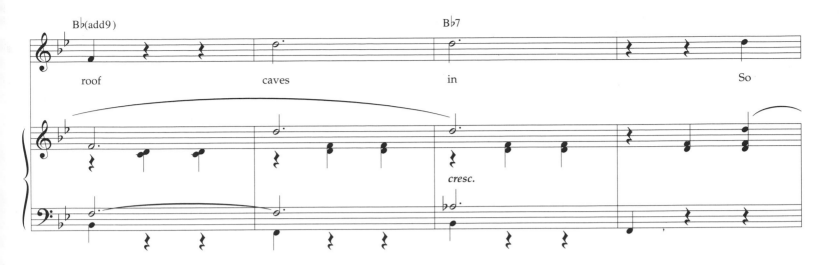

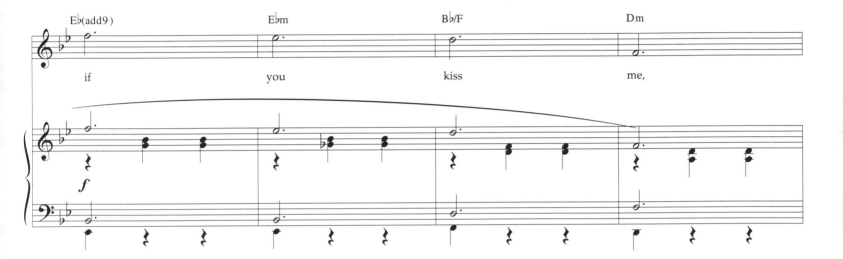

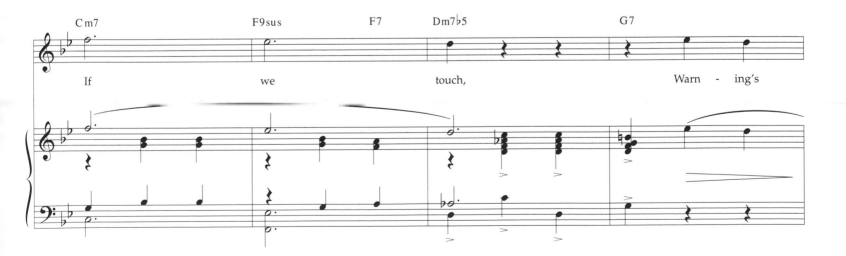

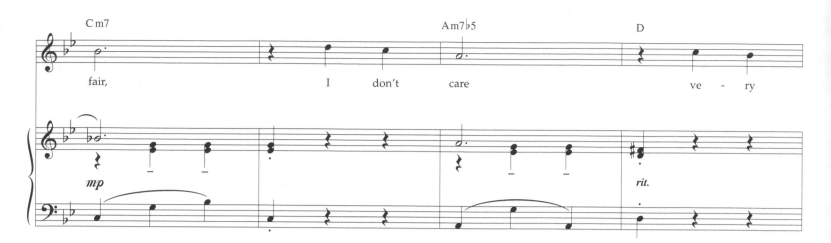

fair, I don't care ve - ry

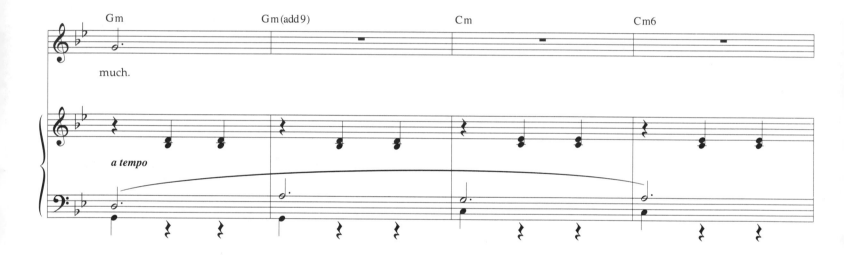

much.

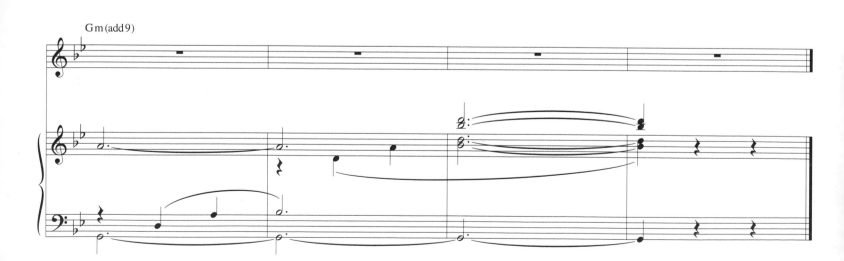

MISTER CELLOPHANE

from *Chicago*

Words by FRED EBB
Music by JOHN KANDER

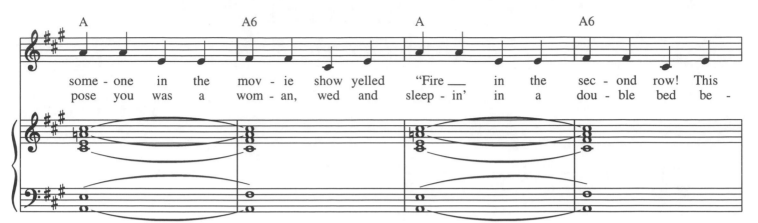

some - one in the mov - ie show yelled "Fire ___ in the sec - ond row! This
pose you was a wom - an, wed and sleep - in' in a dou - ble bed be -

whole place is a pow - der keg!" You'd no - tice him. And
side one man for sev - en years: You'd no - tice him. A

e - ven with-out cluck-ing like a hen,   ev - 'ry-one gets no - ticed now and
hu - man be-ing's made of more than air.   With all that bulk you're bound to see him

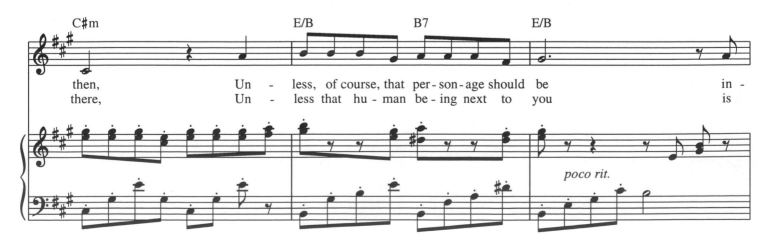

then,   Un - less, of course, that per-son-age should be   in -
there,   Un - less that hu - man be-ing next to you   is

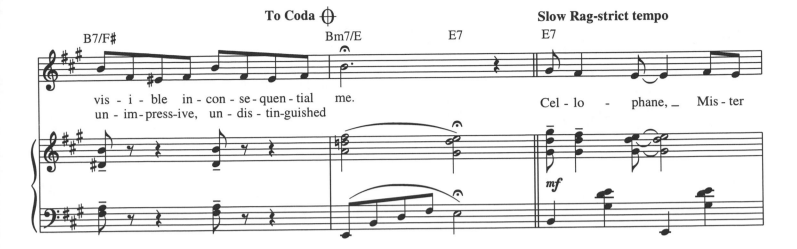

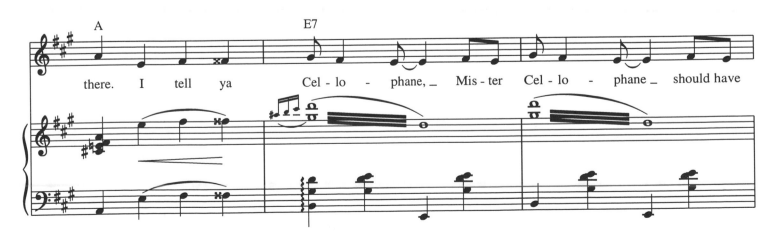

been my name, __ Mis-ter Cel - lo - phane, __ 'cause you can see right thru me,

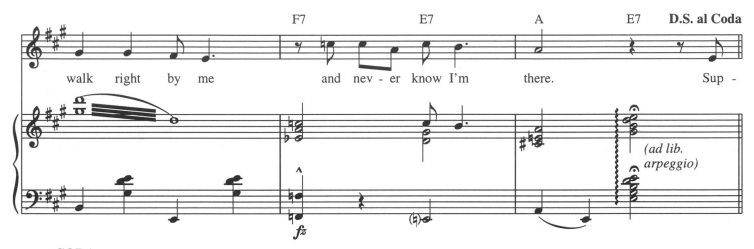

D.S. al Coda

walk right by me and nev - er know I'm there. Sup -

CODA

you know who. Should have

been my name. __ Mis-ter Cel - lo - phane, __ 'cause you can look right thru me, walk with by me,

and nev-er know I'm there. I tell ya Cel-lo-phane, _ Mis-ter Cel-lo - phane _ should have

been my name. _ Mis - ter Cel - lo - phane, _ 'cause you can walk right by me,

look right thru me, and nev-er know I'm there. Nev-er e - ven

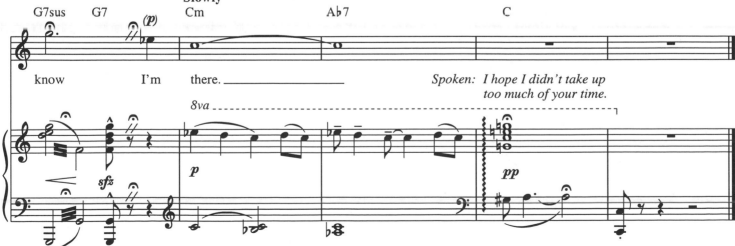

know I'm there. _____

Spoken: I hope I didn't take up too much of your time.

WHAT YOU'D CALL A DREAM
from the Off-Broadway revue *Diamonds*

Music and Lyric by
CRAIG CARNELIA

Slowly and simply ($\downarrow$ = 80)

There are two men out, and it's in the ninth, and the score is four to three. There's a man on first,

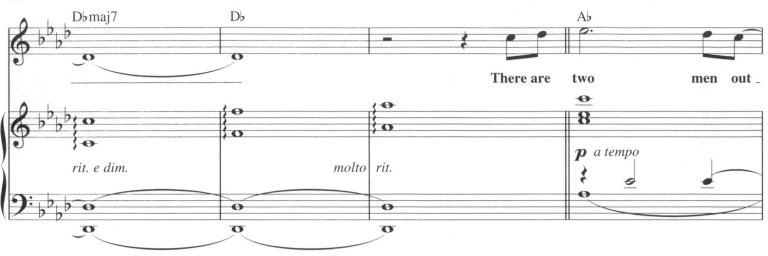

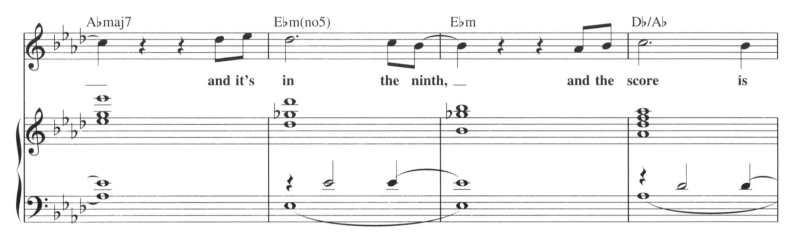

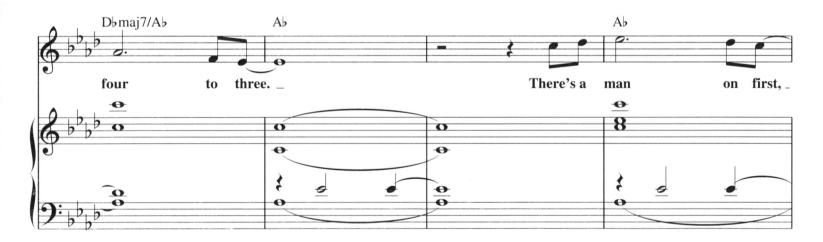

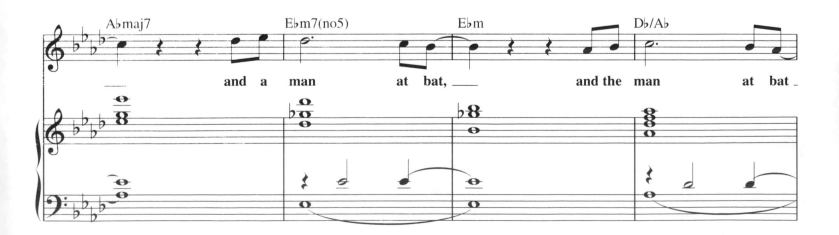

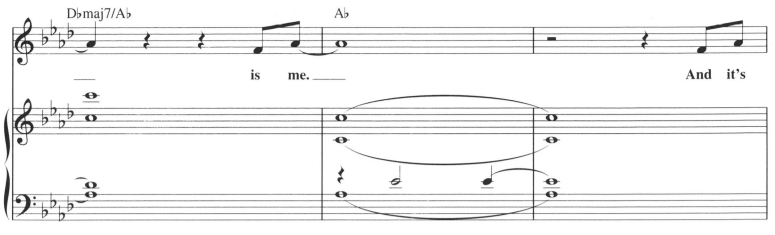

is me. ___ And it's

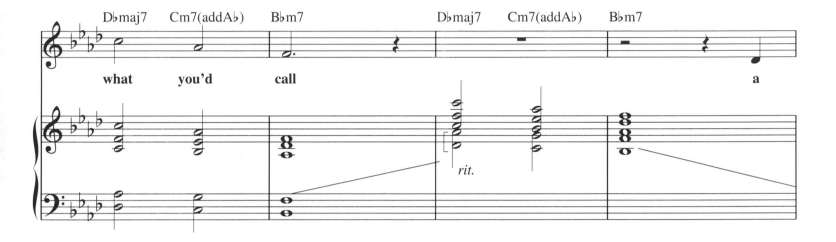

what you'd call a

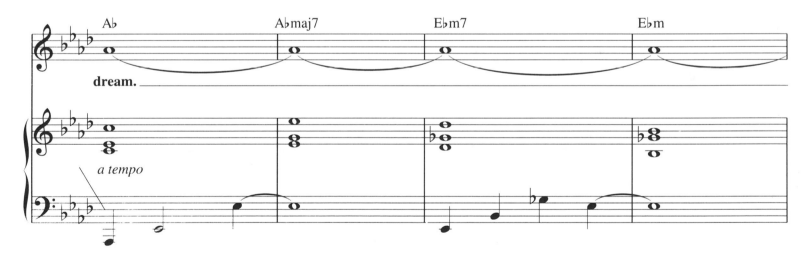

dream. ___

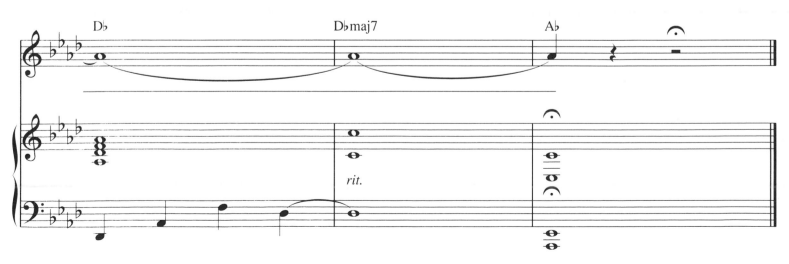

WHAT CAN YOU LOSE

from the Film *Dick Tracy*

Words and Music by
STEPHEN SONDHEIM

What can you lose? _____ On - ly the blues. _

Why keep con-ceal - ing ev - 'ry-thing you're

feel - ing? Say it to her... What can you lose? _____ May - be it shows, _

_ She's had clues, which she chose to ig - nore. _____

poco cresc.

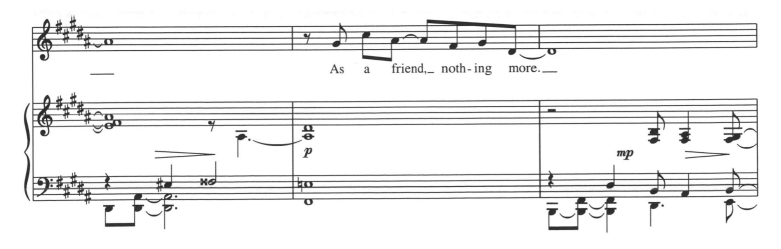

May - be, though, she knows, And just wants _ to go on _ as be - fore. _

dim. *p* *cresc.* *mp*

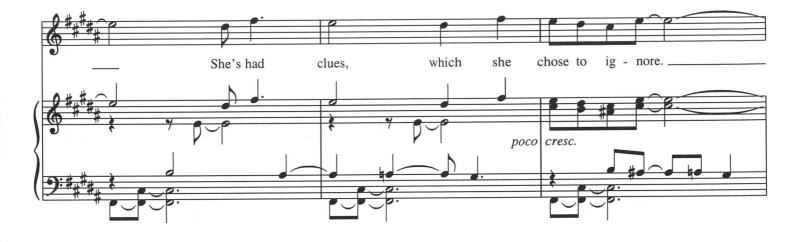

As a friend, _ noth - ing more. _

p *mp*

So she clos - es the door.___ Well, if she does,___ Those are the dues.___ Once the words are spo - ken, Some-thing may be bro - ken. Still, you love her... What can you lose? _____ But what if she goes? _____ At least now,___

you have part__ of her. What if she had__ to choose?__ Leave it a - lone.__

Hold it all in.__

Bet - ter a bone.__ Don't e - ven be - gin.__ With so__ much to

win, There's too much to lose.__

STEPPIN' OUT WITH MY BABY
from the motion picture Irving Berlin's *Easter Parade*

Words and Music by
IRVING BERLIN

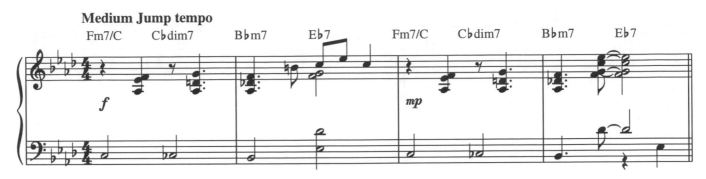

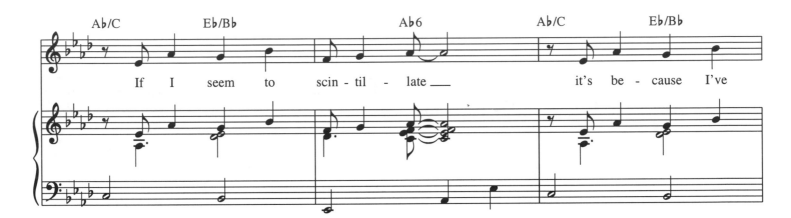

If I seem to scin-til-late ___ it's be-cause I've got a date, ___ a date with a pack-age of ___

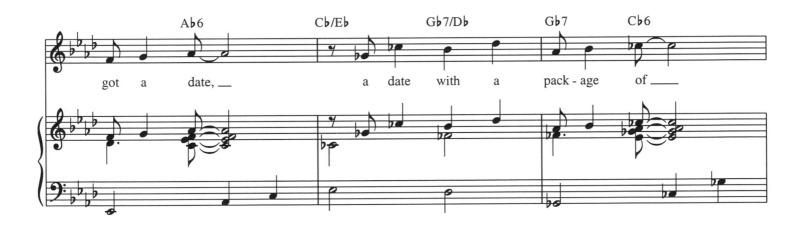

the good things that come with love. ___ You don't have to

ask me, ____ I won't waste your time. But if you should

ask me ___ why I feel sub - lime, I'm ___ step-pin' out ___

with my ba - by. Can't go wrong _ 'cause I'm in right. _ It's for sure, _

not for may - be, that I'm all dressed up to - night. _

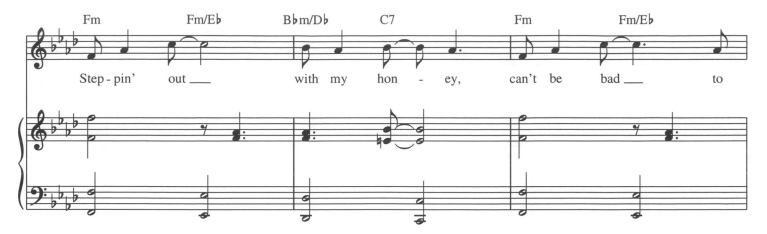

Step-pin' out ___ with my hon - ey, can't be bad ___ to

feel so good. ___ Nev - er felt ___ quite so sun - ny.

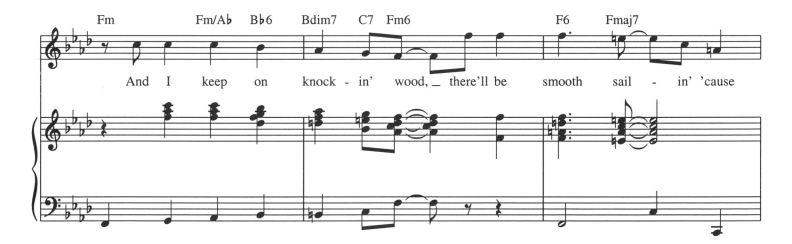

And I keep on knock - in' wood, ___ there'll be smooth sail - in' 'cause

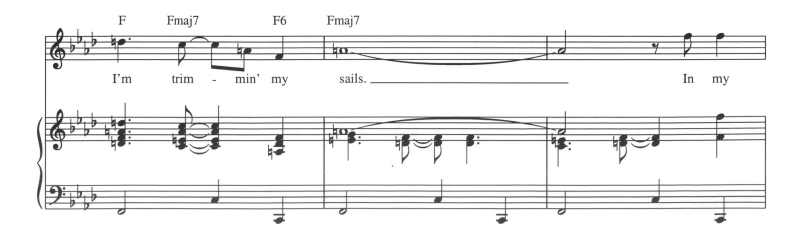

I'm trim - min' my sails. _____ In my

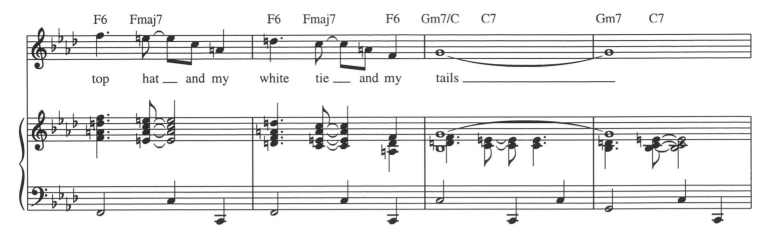

top hat __ and my white tie __ and my tails _____

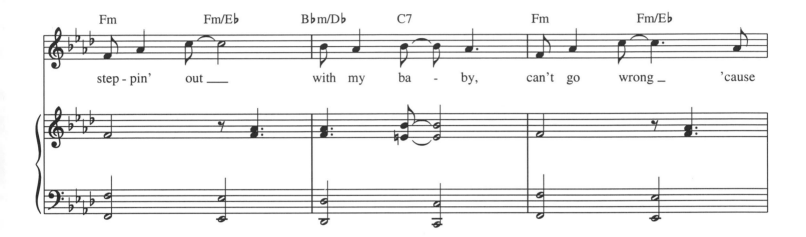

step - pin' out __ with my ba - by, can't go wrong __ 'cause

I'm in right. __ Ask me when __ will the day __ be,

the big day may be to - night. __ be to - night. __

I'M PUTTING ALL MY EGGS IN ONE BASKET

from the motion picture *Follow the Fleet*

Words and Music by
IRVING BERLIN

Moderately (Swing beat)

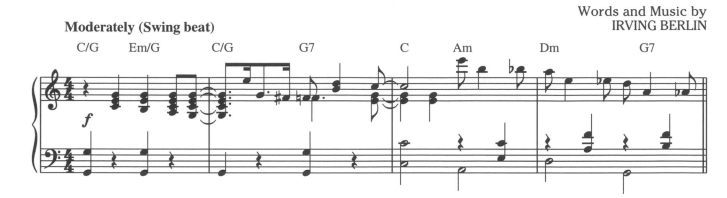

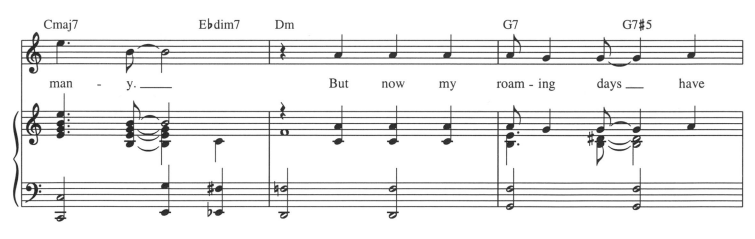

I've been a roam - ing Ro - me - o, ___ my Ju - li - ets ___ have been

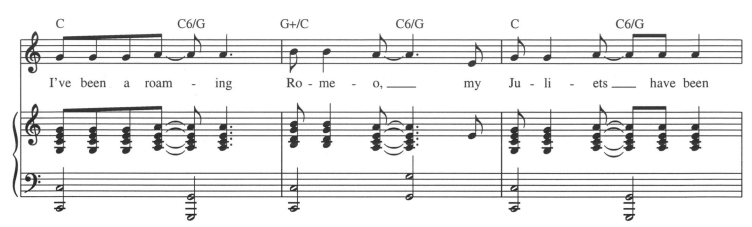

man - y. ___ But now my roam - ing days ___ have

gone. ___ Too man - y i - rons

in the fire ___ is worse than not ___ hav - ing an - y. ___

I've had my share and from ___ now on _____

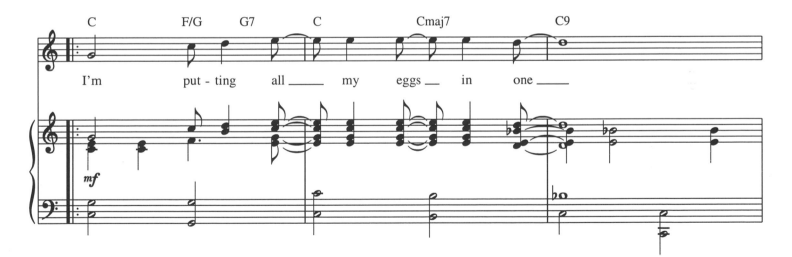

I'm put - ting all ___ my eggs ___ in one ___

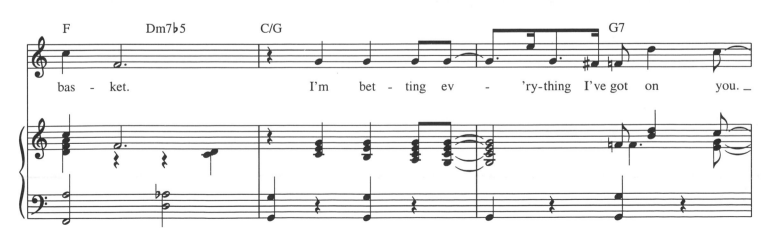

bas - ket. I'm bet - ting ev - 'ry-thing I've got on you. ___

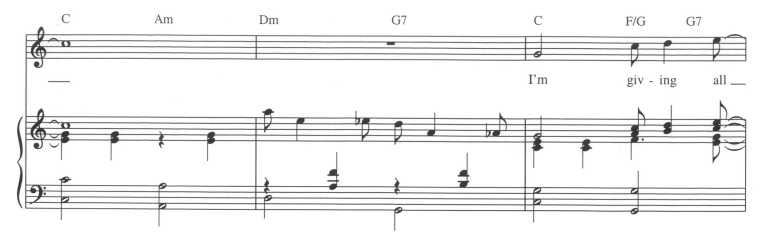

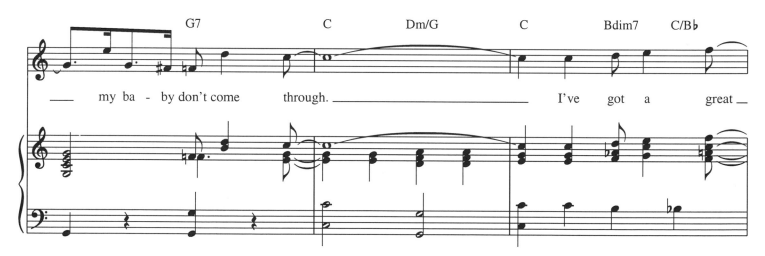

I've de - cid - ed love di - vid - ed in two won't do. So

I'm put - ting all my eggs in one

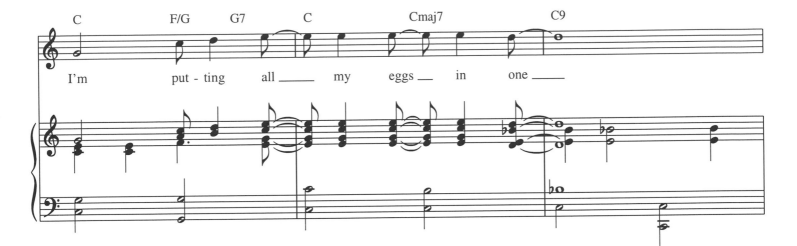

bas - ket. I'm bet - ting ev - 'ry-thing I've got on you.

BUDDY'S BLUES

from *Follies*

Words and Music by
STEPHEN SONDHEIM

Brightly - In 2 (♩ = 92)

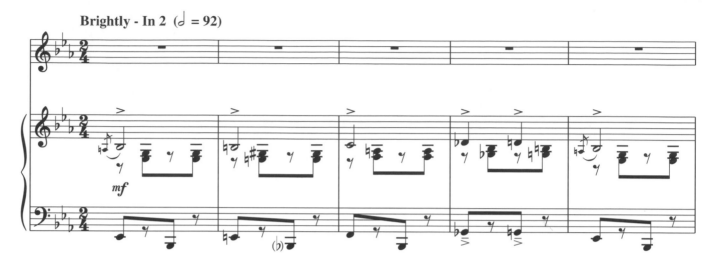

BUDDY:

Hel - lo, folks, ___ we're

in - to the Fol - lies! First, though, folks, ___ we'll pause for a mo'. ___

No, no, folks, ___ you'll still get your jol - lies, It's

just I got a prob-lem that I think you should know. ___

See, I've been ver - y per - turbed ___ of late,

ver - y up - set, ___ Ver - y be - twixt ___ and be - tween. ___

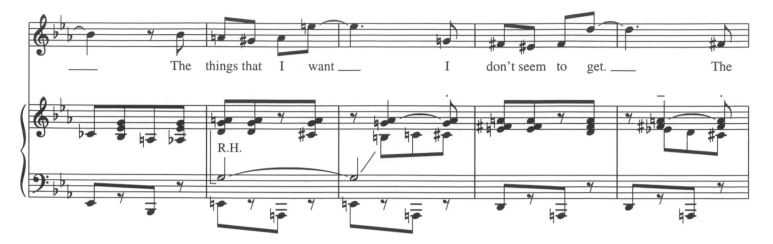

The things that I want ___ I don't seem to get. ___ The

[A la "Looney Tunes"]

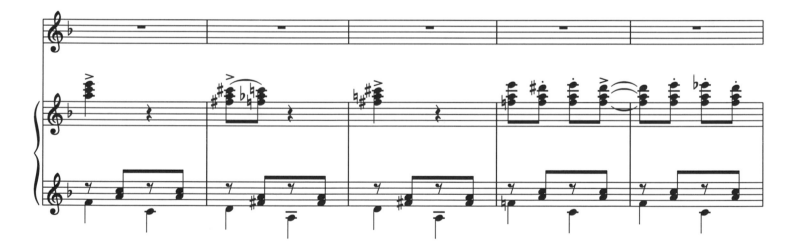

things that I get. . . ___ You know what I mean? ___

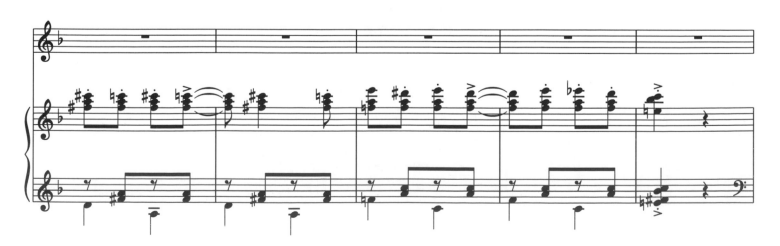

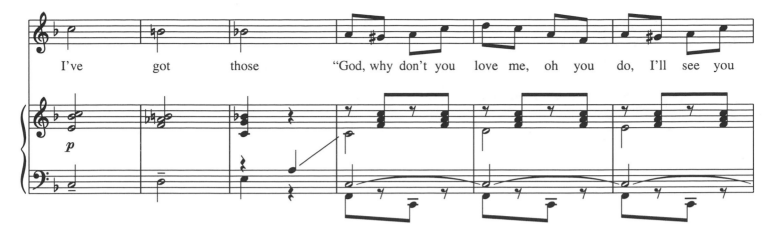

I've got those "God, why don't you love me, oh you do, I'll see you

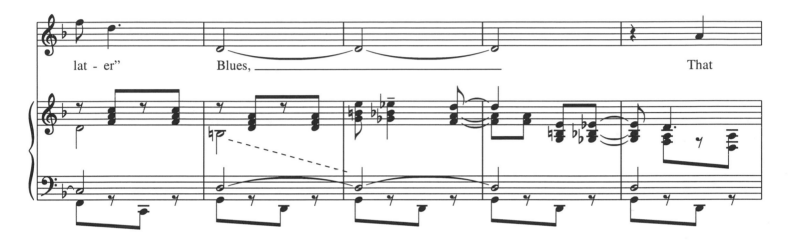

lat - er" Blues, _____ That

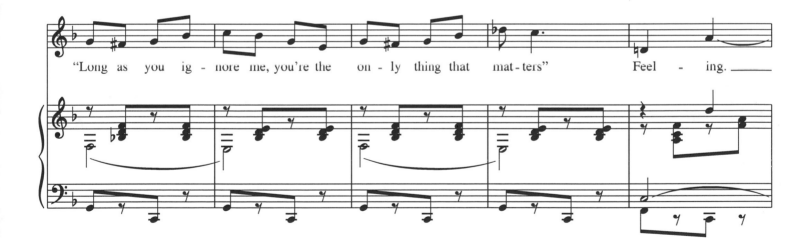

"Long as you ig - nore me, you're the on - ly thing that mat - ters" Feel - ing. _____

_____ That "If I'm good e - nough for you, you're

not good e - nough" And "Thank you for the pres - ent, but what's wrong with it?" stuff.

Those "Don't come an - y clos - er 'cause you know how much I love you"

Feel - ings, Those "Tell me that you

love me, oh you did, I got - ta run now" Blues.

Swingy Four

Spoken: *Margie?*

She says she real-ly loves me, She says. She says she real - ly cares.

* **Margie:**

I love you. I

She says that I'm her he - ro, She says. I'm per-fect, she swears.

care. I care. My he-ro. You're

* It has become customary in stand-alone performances of the song (outside a production) for Buddy to also do "Margie's" part, in falsetto.

She says that if we part-ed, she says, She says that she'd be sick.

per-fect, god-damn it. If we part-ed - - -

She says she's mine for-ev-er, She says. I got-ta get out-

Bleah. For - ev - er.

Tempo primo

- ta here quick! I've got those

Stop-time

"Whis-per how I'm bet-ter than I think, but what do you know?" Blues. _____

_____ That "Why do you keep tell-ing me I

stink when I a - dore you?" Feel - ing. _____ That

"Say I'm all the world to you, you're out of your mind," _ "I know there's some-one

did, now beat it, will you?" Blues. ____

Tempo II°

(Buddy:)

Spoken: Sally. . .   Oh, Sally. . .   She says she loves an-oth-er,

* Sally:

An-

She says, A fel - la she pre - fers.   She says that he's her i-dol.

- oth-er.   Furs.   furs.

* *As before, Buddy can do Sally's part in falsetto.*

die! _____ I've got those

"God, why don't you love me, oh you do, I'll see you lat-er" Blues,

* **Girls:** *(falsetto)*
Bla bla blues, ___

Buddy:
That "Long as you ig-nore me, you're the

on-ly thing that mat-ters" Feel - ing.

* **Girls:** *(falsetto)* Feel - ing.

Feel - ing. _____

gliss.

* *These "Girls" lines in falsetto are optional.*

MAKE THE MOST OF YOUR MUSIC

from *Follies*

Words and Music by
STEPHEN SONDHEIM

74

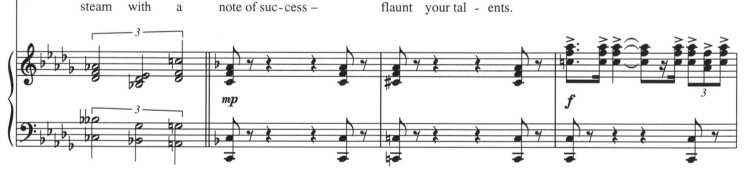

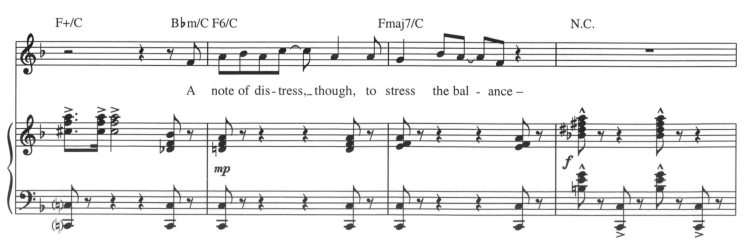

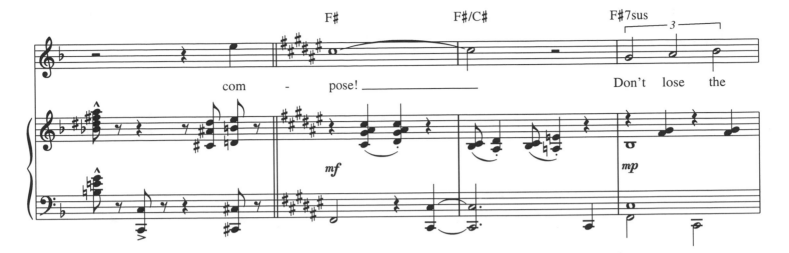

note of guile, _

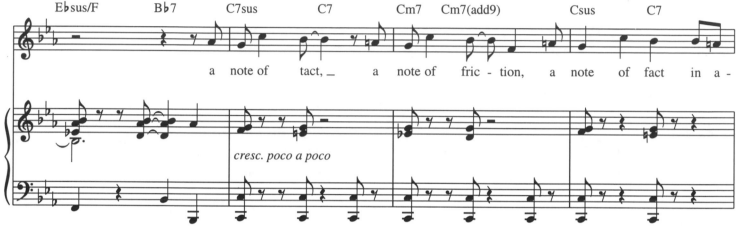

a note of tact, _ a note of fric - tion, a note of fact in a -

cresc. poco a poco

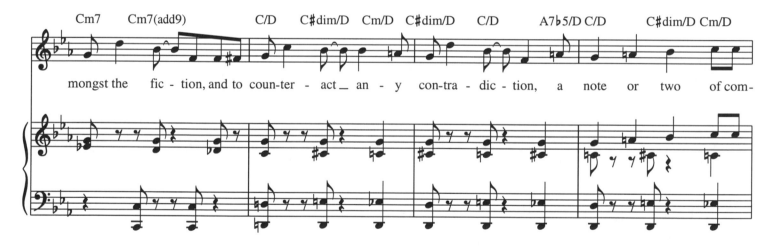

mongst the fic - tion, and to coun-ter - act _ an - y con-tra - dic - tion, a note or two of com-

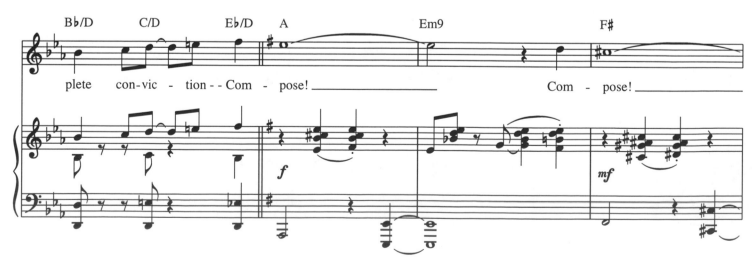

plete con-vic - tion - - Com - pose! _____ Com - pose! _____

f

mf

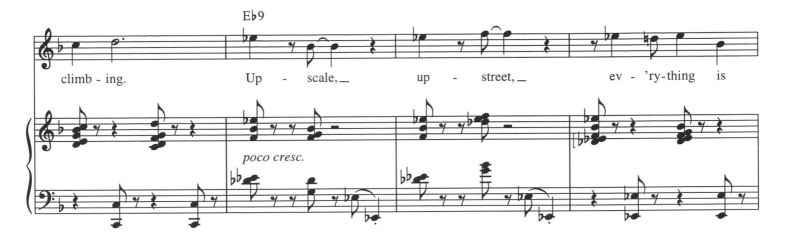

climb - ing. Up - scale,— up - street,— ev - 'ry-thing is

poco cresc.

tim - ing...

cresc.

Comes the — day, —— all too — soon, ——

mf

when you — may —— have to trust your — tune. ——

Make the ___ most ___ of your mu - sic and, who

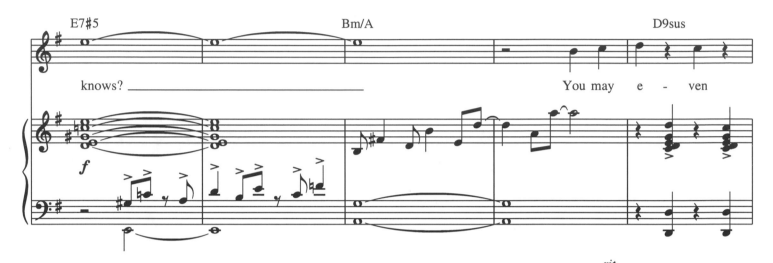

knows? _____ You may e - ven

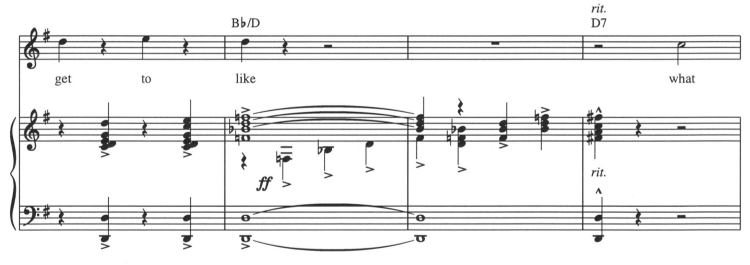

get to like what

you com - pose! _____

MAMA SAYS
from the Broadway musical *Footloose*

Words by DEAN PITCHFORD
Music by TOM SNOW

With a bayou beat

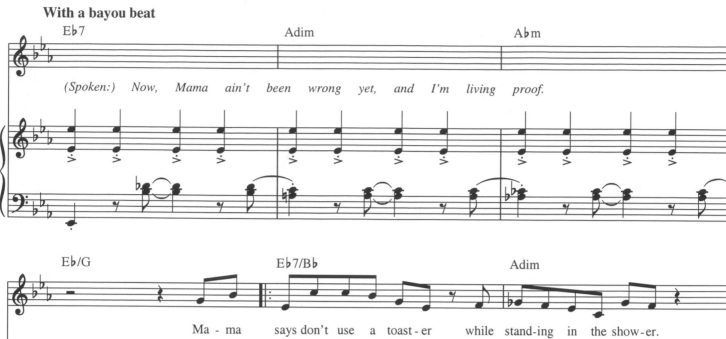

(Spoken:) Now, Mama ain't been wrong yet, and I'm living proof.

Ma - ma says don't use a toast - er while stand-ing in the show-er.
says don't drink hot cof - fee ly - ing down in bed. __

Now who can ar - gue with that? ____ Ma - ma says don't hold your breath for
Don't e - ven give it a thought. __ Ma - ma says nev - er eat an - y-thing that's

long - er than an ho - ur. The wom-an knows_ where it's at! __ ⎫
big - ger than your head. __ Is she a whiz_ or what? __ ⎭

And Ma-ma says _

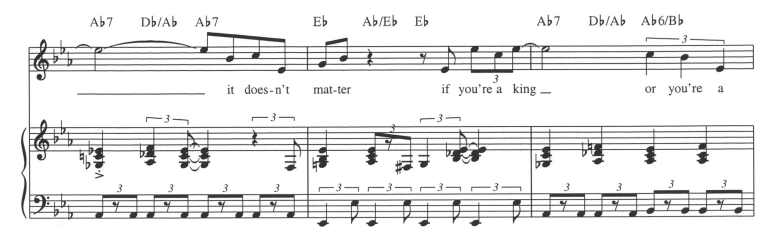

it does-n't mat-ter if you're a king ___ or you're a

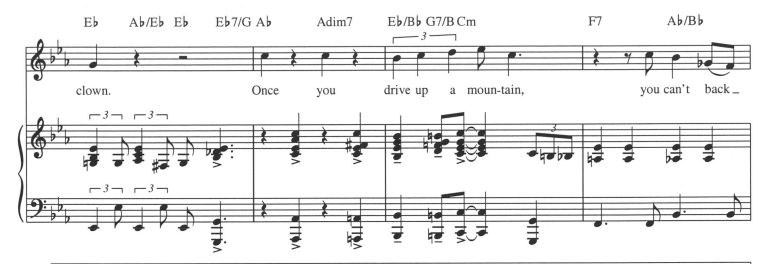

clown. Once you drive up a moun-tain, you can't back ___

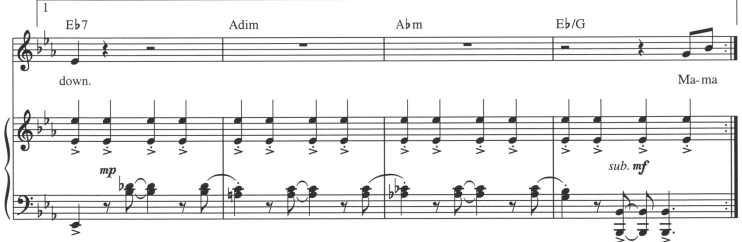

down. Ma-ma

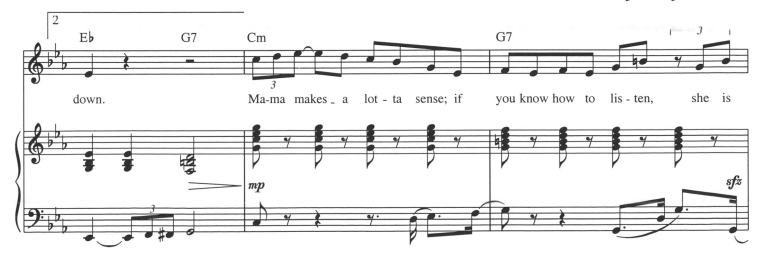

down. Ma-ma makes ___ a lot-ta sense; if you know how to lis-ten, she is

clear _____ and con - cise. _____ Dad-dy says,_ "I love her, son,_ but

she's got mar-bles miss-in'." But I say, "Hey!_ It's free ad - vice,_ and what d' you ex-pect at that

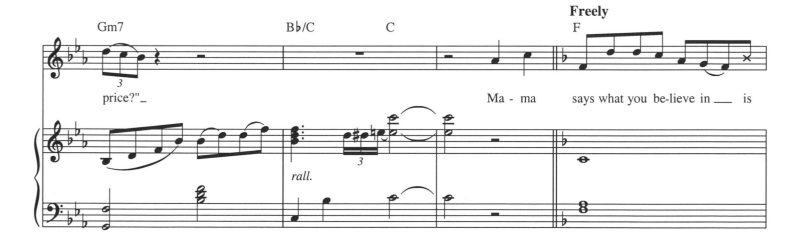

Freely

price?"_ Ma - ma says what you be-lieve in ___ is

all you real-ly own,_ and I be-lieve that she's right. Ma - ma says if you've got doubts,_ well then,

A tempo

boy, you're not a-lone.___ Just means you're read - y to fight.___ And Ma-ma says___

___ it does-n't mat-ter if you're a king or you're a

clown. Once you drive up a moun-tain,

you can't back___ down. You can turn up the heat, you can

Once you drive up a moun - tain, you can't back

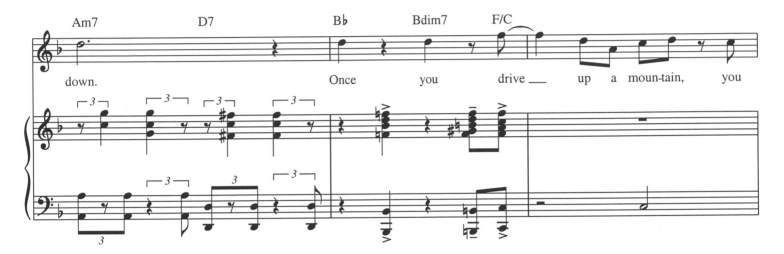

down. Once you drive ___ up a moun-tain, you

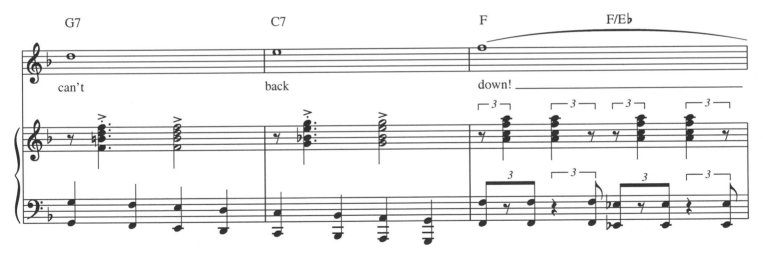

can't back down! _____

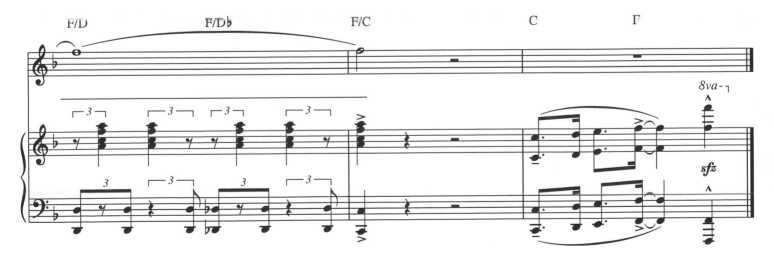

I CAN'T STAND STILL

from the Broadway musical *Footloose*

Words by DEAN PITCHFORD
Music by TOM SNOW

Moderate 16th note Funk

I nev-er walk when I can run, I don't be-lieve I ev-er could.
I called the doc-tor; he said, "Son, I can-not of-fer you a pill."

Peo-ple try to slow me down, Say-ing, "Boy, you real-ly should
So I nev-er found re-lief and now I've got to move un-til

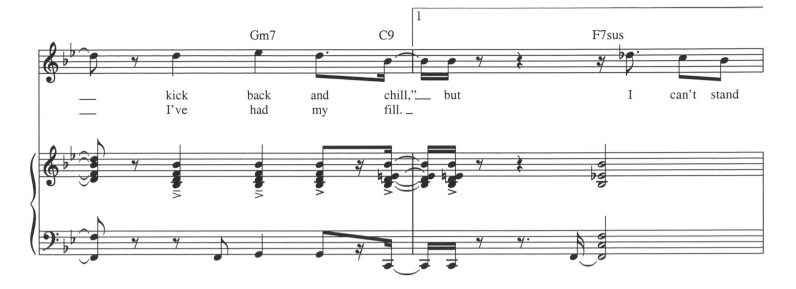

kick   back   and   chill,"___ but   I   can't   stand
I've   had   my   fill. ___

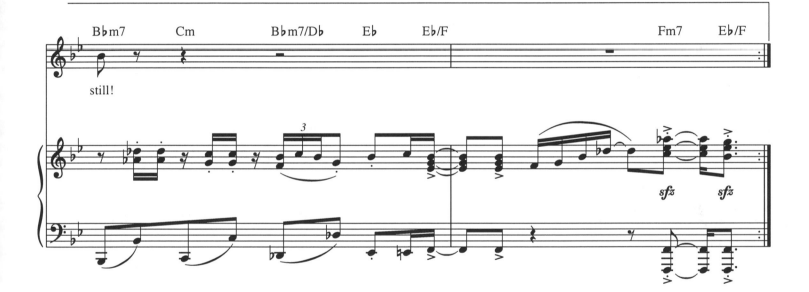

still!

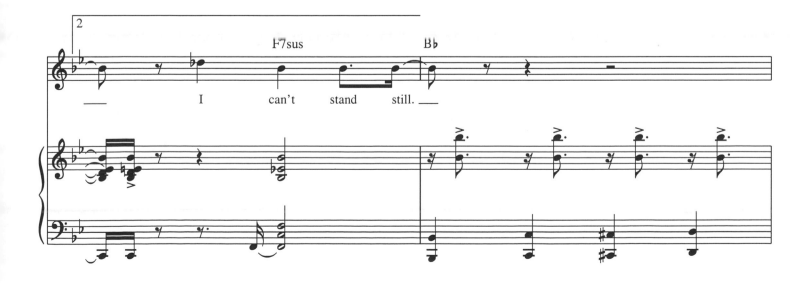

___   I   can't   stand   still. ___

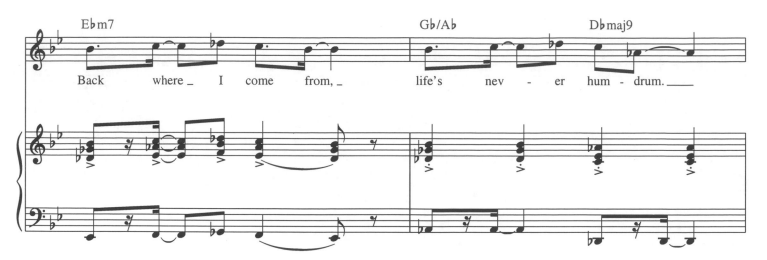

Back where I come from, life's nev-er hum-drum.

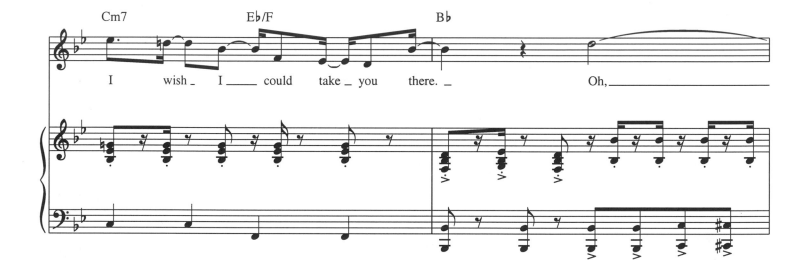

I wish I could take you there. Oh,

we had the world at our feet. Life was

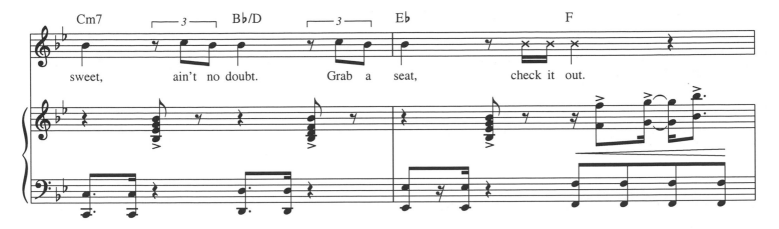

sweet,   ain't no doubt.   Grab a   seat,   check it out.

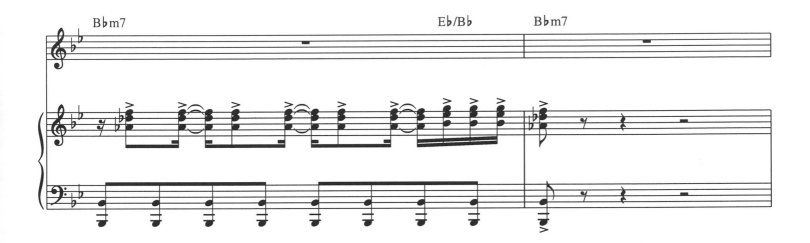

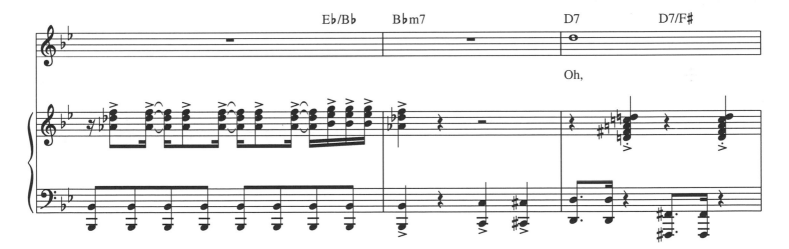

Oh,

I thought it nev - er would end. _____   But I   lost   it   some - how. _____   Would you

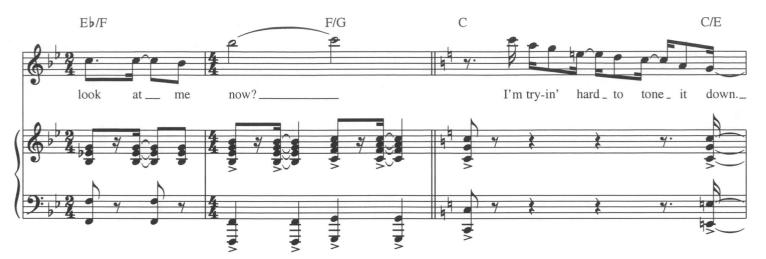

look at __ me now? _____ I'm try-in' hard __ to tone __ it down. __

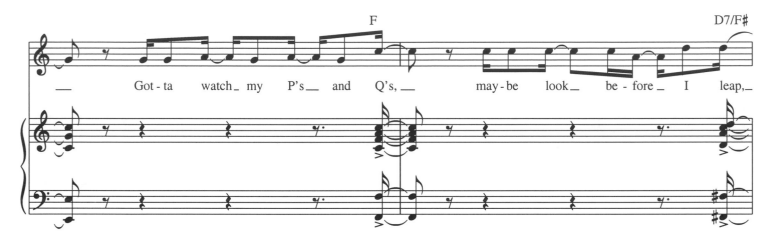

__ Got-ta watch __ my P's __ and Q's, __ may-be look __ be-fore __ I leap, __

__ and then I think, __ "Hey, what's __ the use?" __ Ain't done it yet, __

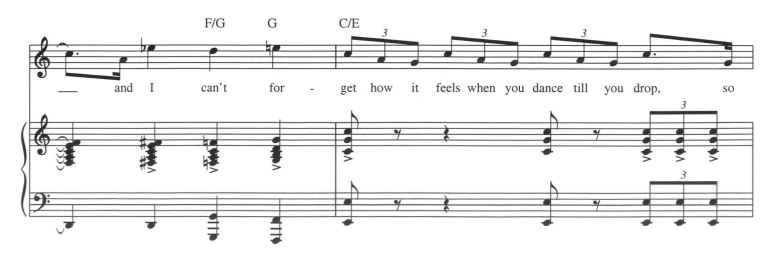

__ and I can't for - get how it feels when you dance till you drop, so

TAKE A PAIR OF SPARKLING EYES
from *The Gondoliers*

Words by W.S. GILBERT
Music by ARTHUR SULLIVAN

Allegretto moderato

MARCO:

1. Take a pair of spar-kling eyes, _____ Hid-den, ev-er and a-non, _____ In a
2. Take a pret-ty lit-tle cot-_____ Quite a min-ia-ture af-fair-_____ Hung a-

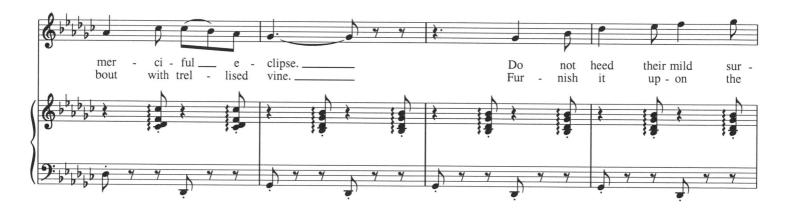

mer-ci-ful_____ e-clipse. _____ Do not heed their mild sur-
bout with trel-lised vine. _____ Fur-nish it up-on the

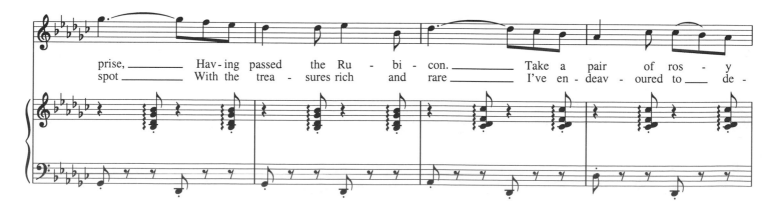

prise, _____ Hav-ing passed the Ru-bi-con. _____ Take a pair of ros-y
spot _____ With the trea-sures rich and rare _____ I've en-deav-oured to_____ de-

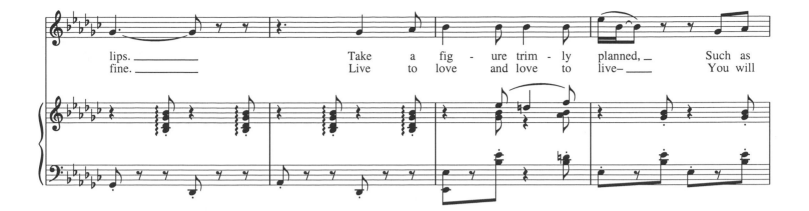

lips. _____
fine. _____

Take a fig-ure trim-ly planned, _ Such as
Live to love and love to live– _ You will

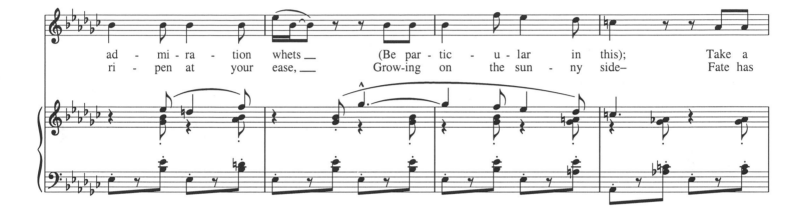

ad - mi - ra - tion whets _ (Be par - tic - u - lar in this); Take a
ri - pen at your ease, _ Grow-ing on the sun - ny side– Fate has

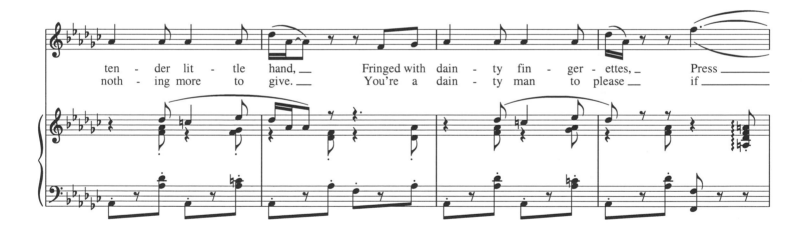

ten - der lit - tle hand, _ Fringed with dain - ty fin - ger - ettes, _ Press _____
noth - ing more to give. _ You're a dain - ty man to please _ if _____

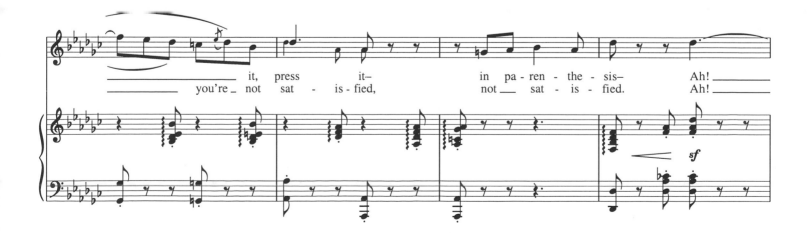

_____ it, press it– in pa - ren - the - sis– Ah! _____
_____ you're not sat - is - fied, not sat - is - fied. Ah! _____

sf

Take _____ all these, you luck - y
Take _____ my coun - sel, hap - py

man— _____ Take and keep them, if ___ you can, if ___ you can! Take all
man; _____ Act up - on it, if ___ you can, if ___ you can! Take my

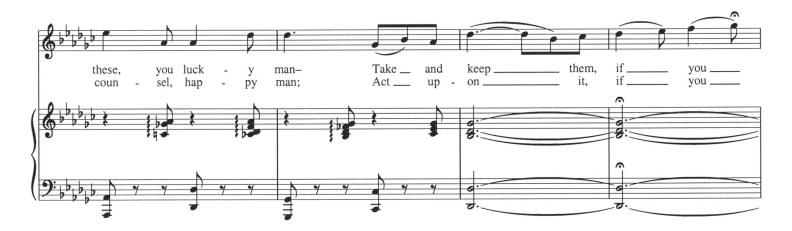

these, you luck - y man— Take ___ and keep _____ them, if _____ you ___
coun - sel, hap - py man; Act ___ up - on _____ it, if _____ you ___

can, if _____ you can! _____
can, if _____ you can! _____

Take my coun - sel, hap - py man!

Act up - on it, if you can, if you can, if you

cresc.   *f*   *con forza*

can, Act up - on it, if you can,_____ hap - py man,

if _____ you can! _____

GO THE DISTANCE
from Walt Disney Pictures' *Hercules*

Music by ALAN MENKEN
Lyrics by DAVID ZIPPEL

Moderate Ballad

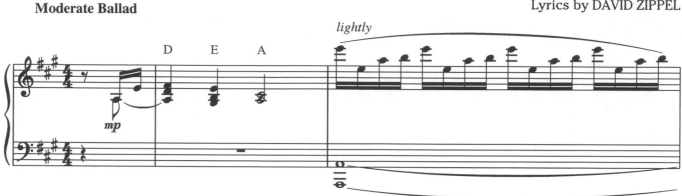

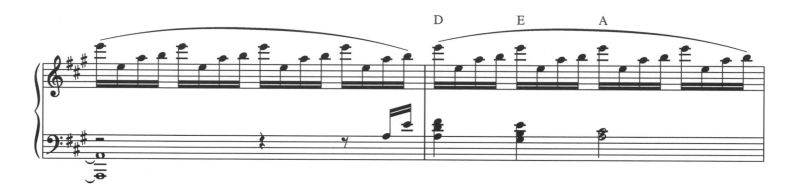

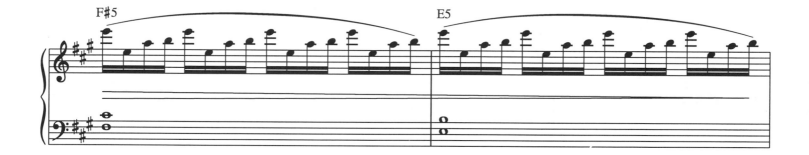

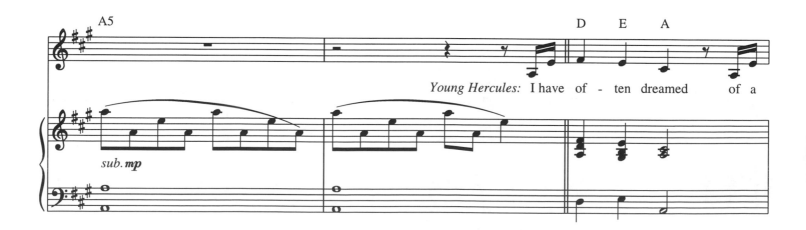

Young Hercules: I have of - ten dreamed of a

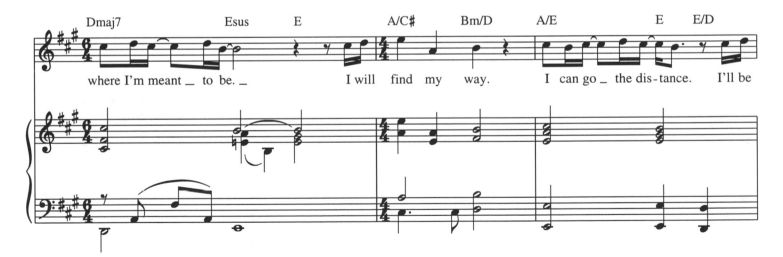

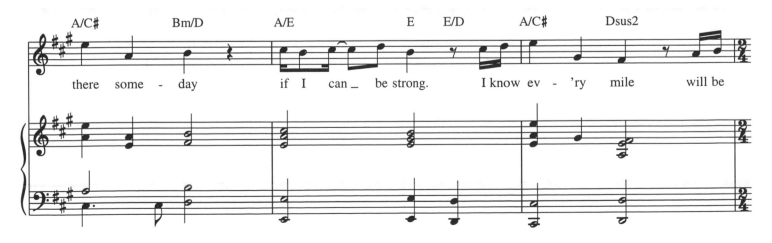

worth my ___ while. I would go most an-y-where to

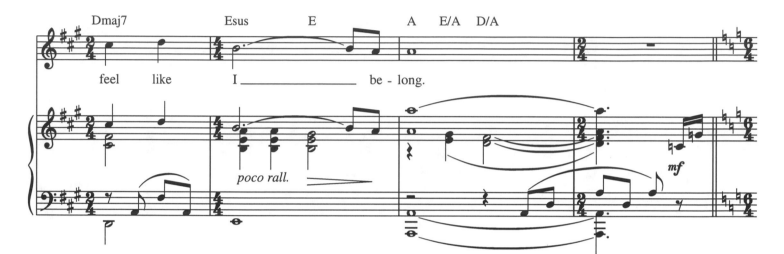

feel like I _____ be - long.

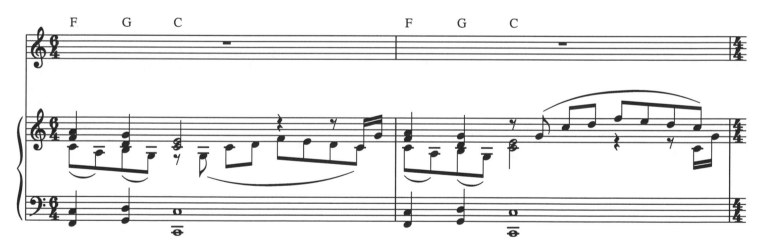

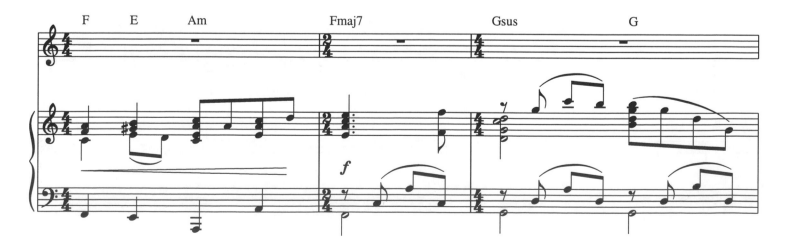

AMSTERDAM

from *Jacques Brel Is Alive and Well and Living in Paris*

French Words and Music by JACQUES BREL
English Words by MORT SHUMAN
and ERIC BLAU

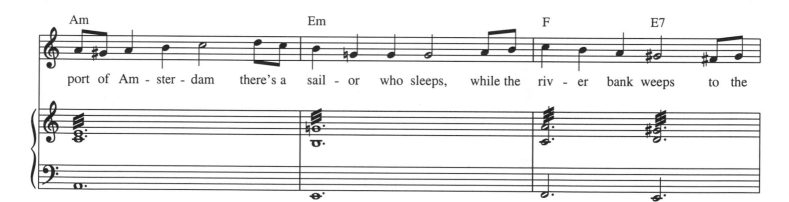

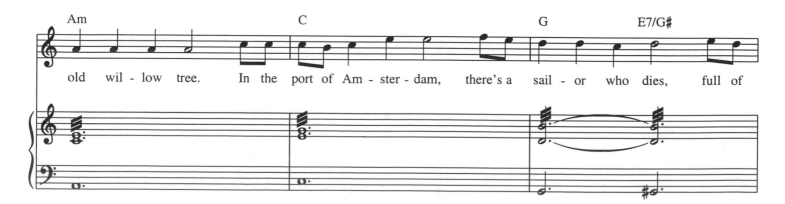

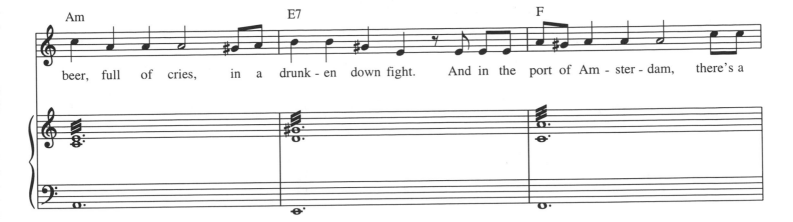

beer, full of cries, in a drunk - en down fight. And in the port of Am - ster - dam, there's a

sail - or who's born on a mug - gy hot morn, by the dawn's ear - ly light. In the

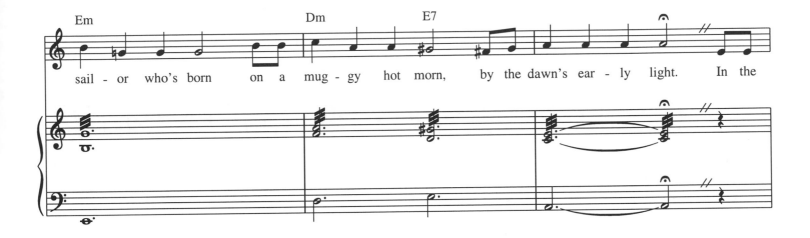

port of Am - ster - dam, where the sail - ors all meet, there's a sail - or who eats on - ly

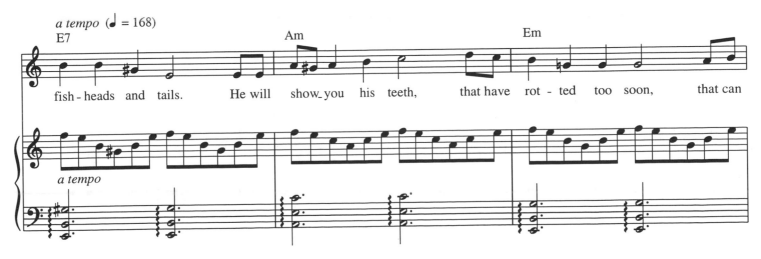

fish - heads and tails. He will show you his teeth, that have rot - ted too soon, that can

swal-low the moon, that can haul up the sails. And he yells_ to the cook with his

arms o - pen wide, "Bring me more fish, put it down by my side." He

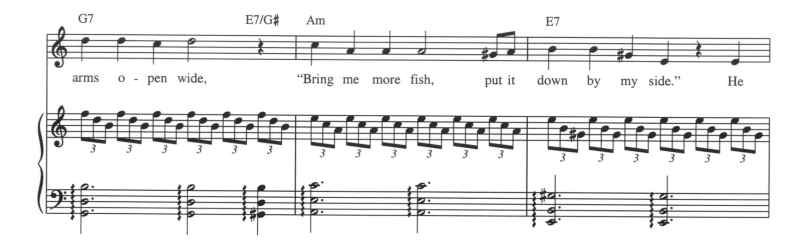

wants_so to belch, but he's too full to try, so he gets up and laughs and he

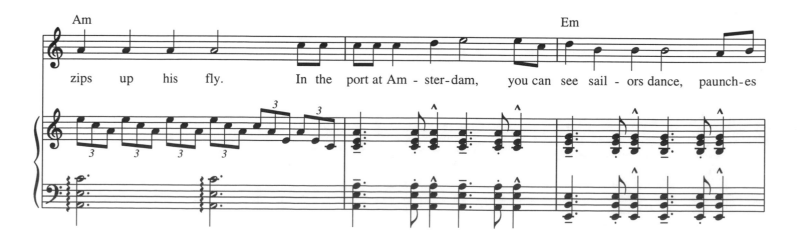

zips up his fly. In the port at Am - ster-dam, you can see sail - ors dance, paunch-es

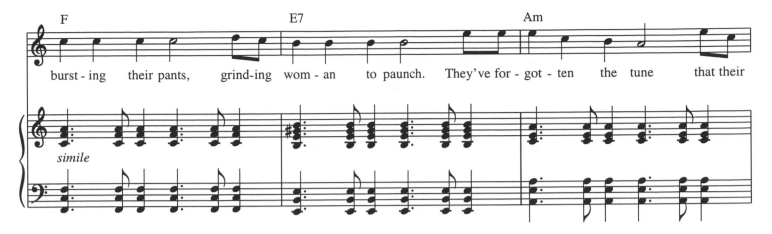

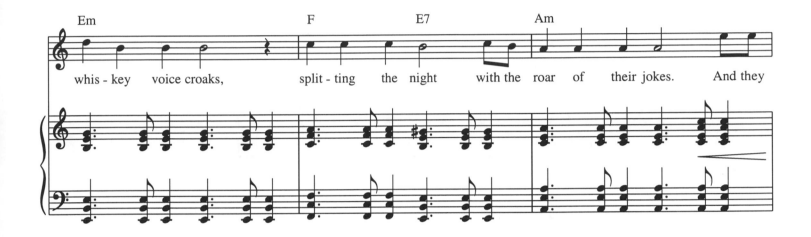

pride in their pants, with the slut that they tow un-der-neath the street lamps. In the

port of Am-ster-dam, there's a sail-or who drinks, and he drinks and he drinks and he

drinks once a-gain. He drinks to the health of the whores of Am-ster-dam, who have

prom-ised their love to a thou-sand oth-er men. They've_

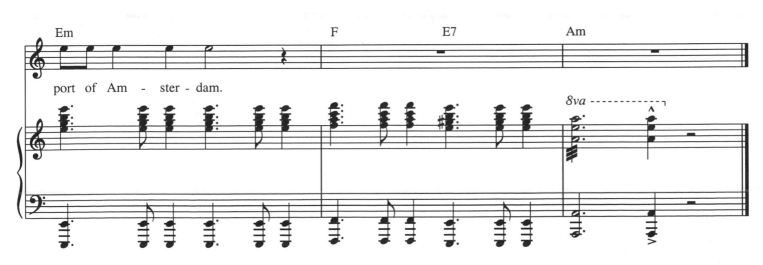

ALIVE!
from *Jekyll & Hyde*

Words by LESLIE BRICUSSE
Music by FRANK WILDHORN

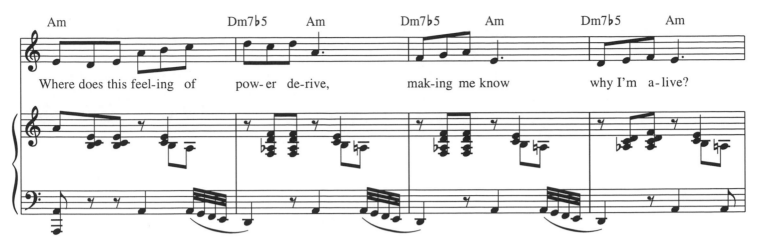

Where does this feel-ing of pow-er de-rive, mak-ing me know why I'm a-live?

Like the night, it's a se-cret _____ sin-is-ter dark and un-known.

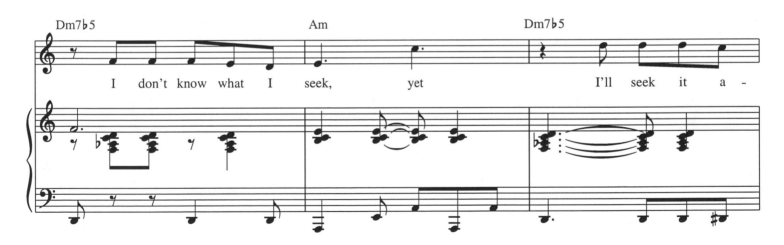

I don't know what I seek, yet I'll seek it a-

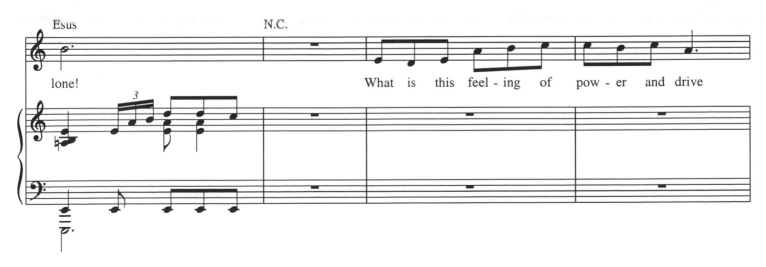

lone! What is this feel-ing of pow-er and drive

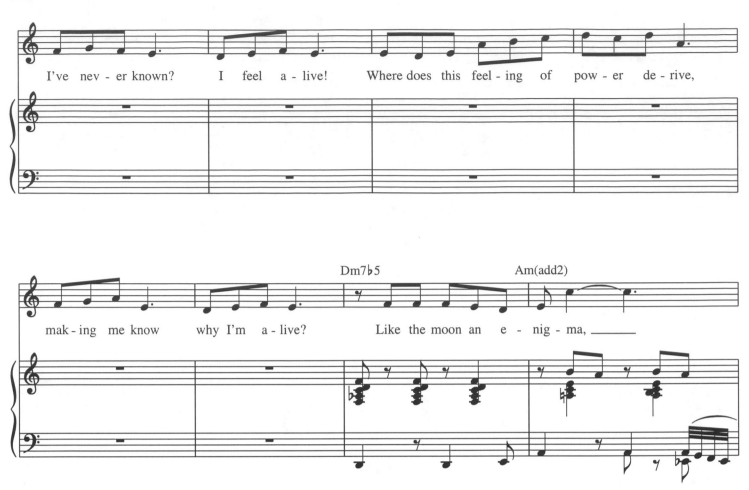

I've nev - er known? I feel a - live! Where does this feel - ing of pow - er de - rive,

mak - ing me know why I'm a - live? Like the moon an e - nig - ma, _____

lost and a - lone in the night. Damned by some heav - en - ly stig - ma but

blaz - ing ___ with light. It's the feel - ing of

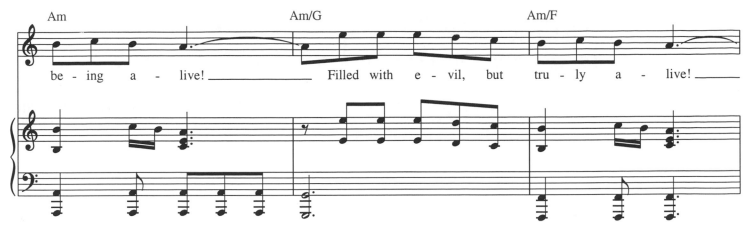

be - ing a - live! ___ Filled with e - vil, but tru - ly a - live! ___

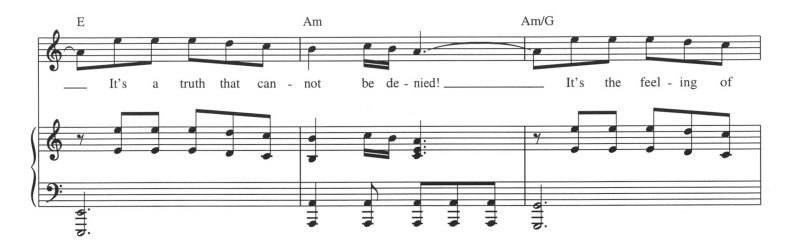

___ It's a truth that can - not be de - nied! ___ It's the feel - ing of

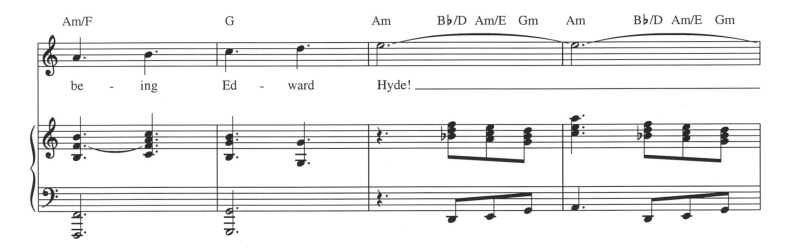

be - ing Ed - ward Hyde! _____

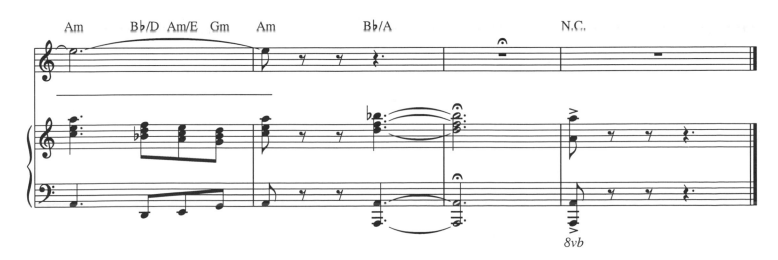

ANY DREAM WILL DO

from *Joseph and the Amazing Technicolor® Dreamcoat*

Music by ANDREW LLOYD WEBBER
Lyrics by TIM RICE

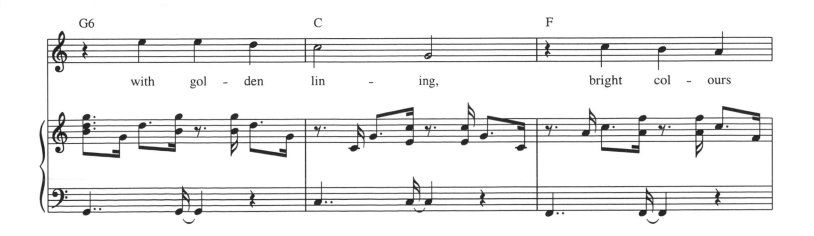

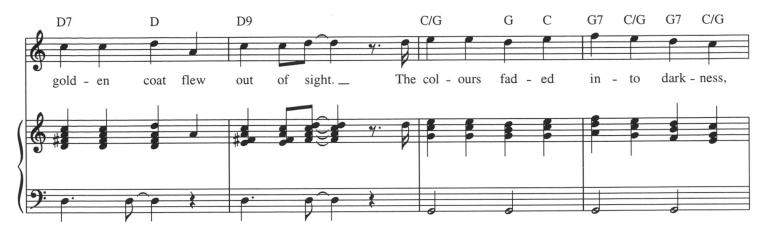

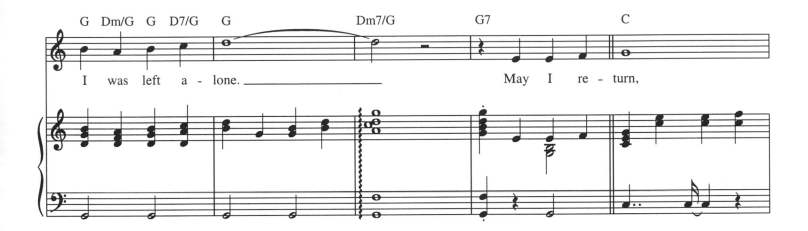

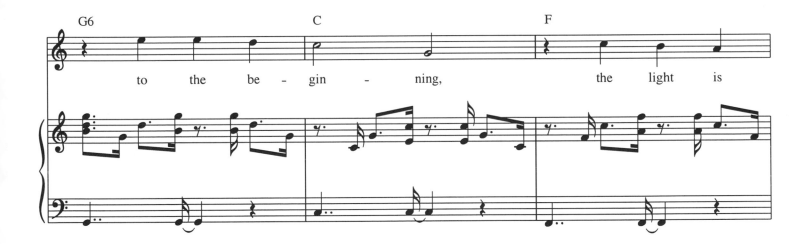

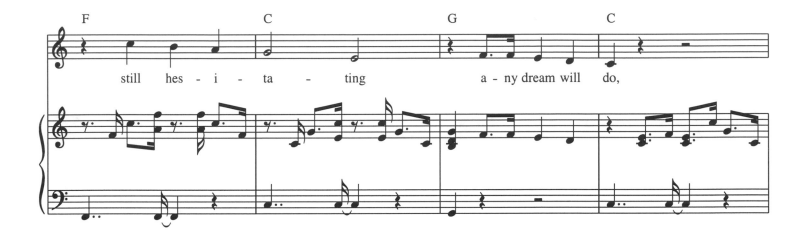

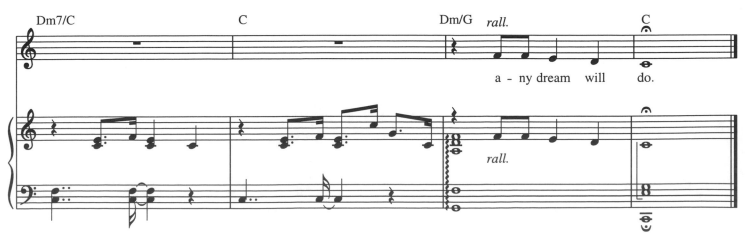

I'M MARTIN GUERRE

from *Martin Guerre*

Music by CLAUDE-MICHEL SCHÖNBERG
Lyrics by ALAIN BOUBLIL and STEPHEN CLARK

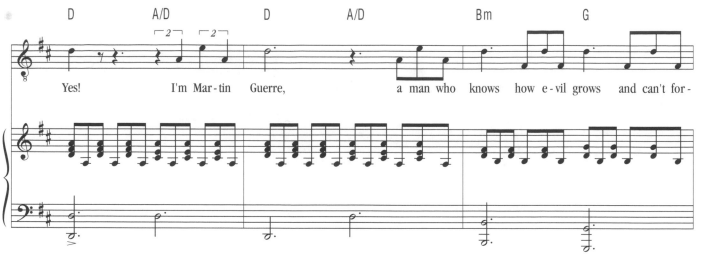

Yes! I'm Mar-tin Guerre, a man who knows how e-vil grows and can't for-

give. Soon_____ they will see_____ a

man can choose to___ be free. They all_____ look for some-one to

blame but I swear it a-loud, I___will be proud that___Mar-tin Guerre_____ is my

blame   but I swear it a - loud, I___ will be proud I'm___ Mar - tin Guerre.   They

all   look for some - one to blame   but I swear it a - loud, I___ will be proud that___ Mar - tin

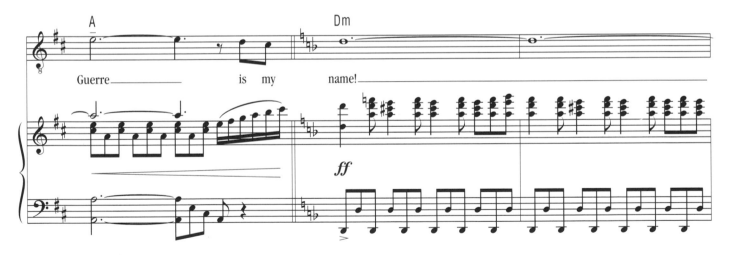

Guerre_____ is my name!___

NIGHT OF MY NIGHTS

from *Kismet*

Words and Music by ROBERT WRIGHT
and GEORGE FORREST
(Music Based on Themes by A. Borodin)

CALIPH:

Play on the cym - bal, the tim - bal, the ly - re, Play with ap - pro - pri - ate pas - sion; fash - ion Songs of de -

light and de - li - cious de - sire ____ For the

night of my nights! _____

Come where the so well be - lov - ed is

wait - ing, where the rose and the jas - mine

min - gle, while I tell her the moon is for

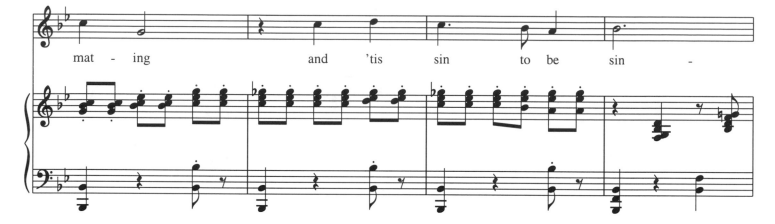

mat - ing and 'tis sin to be sin -

gle! _____ Let pea - cocks and

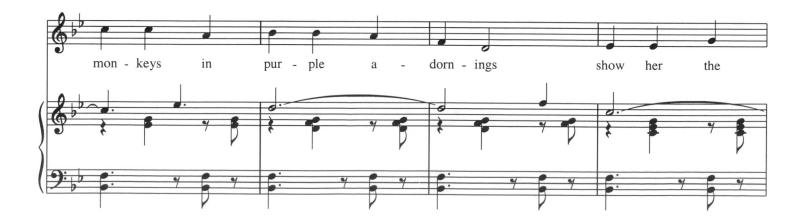

mon - keys in pur - ple a - dorn - ings show her the

way to my bri - dal cham - ber, then get you gone ____

____ till the morn of my morn - ings af - ter the

night of my nights. _____ Af - ter the

night of my nights! _____ 'Tis the

night of my nights! _____ Ah! _____

Fash - ion songs of de -

light and de - li - cious de - sire. _____

For the night of my nights! _____

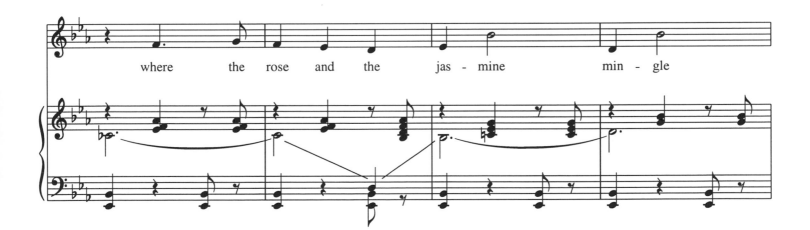

Come where the so well be - lov - ed is wait - ing,

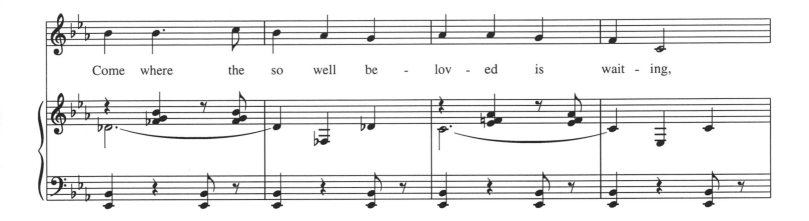

where the rose and the jas - mine min - gle

While I tell her the moon is for - mat - ing.

And 'tis sin to be sin - gle! _____

_____ Let pea - cocks and mon - keys in pur - ple a -

mf

dorn - ings Show her the way to my bri - dal

cham - ber, Then get you gone till the morn of my morn - ings

Af - ter the night of my nights! _____ 'Tis the

night of my nights! _____

'Tis the night of my nights! _____

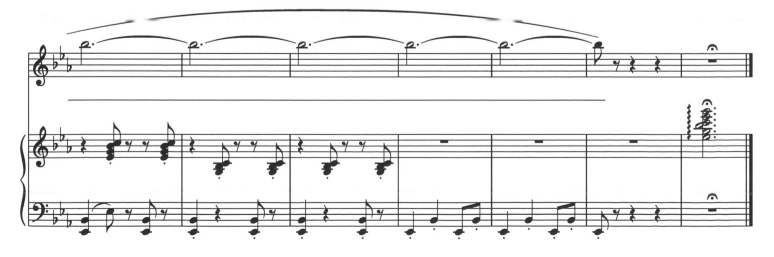

HEY THERE

from *The Pajama Game*

Words and Music by RICHARD ADLER
and JERRY ROSS

Slowly and expressively (♩ = 90)

mf

SID:
p
mp

Hey there, _____ you with the stars in your eyes, Love nev-er made a

fool of you, You used to be too wise! _____

Hey there, _____ you on that high fly-ing cloud. Though she won't throw a

crumb to you, You think some-day, she'll come to you;_____ Bet-ter for-

get her, _____ Her with her nose in the air. She has you danc - ing

on a string, Break it and she won't care! _____ Won't you

take this ad-vice I hand you like a broth-er _____ Or are you

not see-ing things too clear, Are you just too far gone to hear, Is it

all go-ing in one ear and out the oth - er Bet - ter for -

get her, _____ Her with her nose in the air!

A pup - pet on a string! She won't

care for me! Take this ad-vice I hand you like a broth-er?____

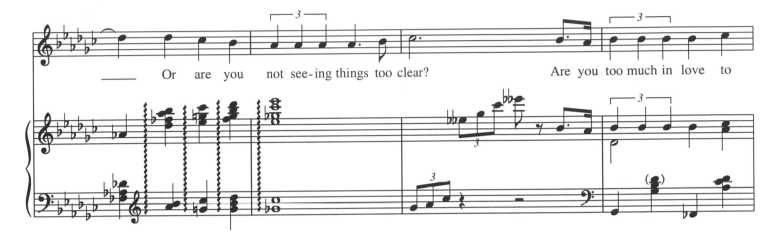

____ Or are you not see-ing things too clear? Are you too much in love to

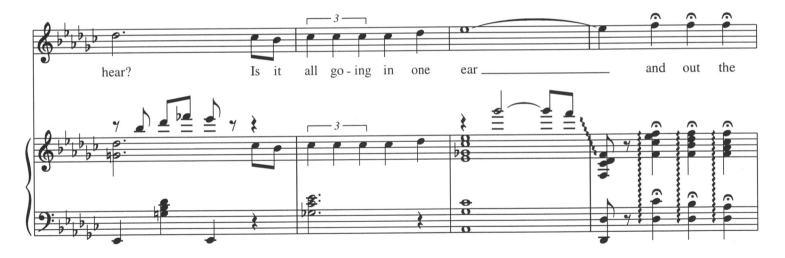

hear? Is it all go-ing in one ear____ and out the

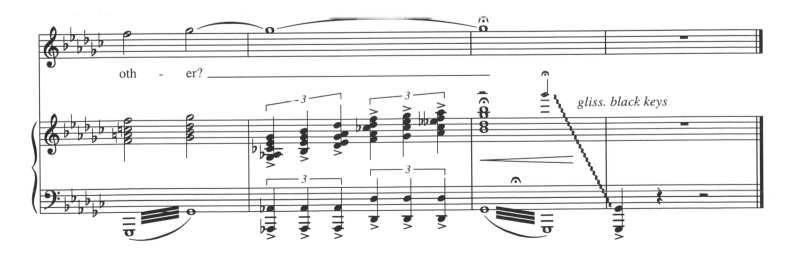

oth - er?____

gliss. black keys

THE OLD RED HILLS OF HOME

from *Parade*

Music and Lyrics by
JASON ROBERT BROWN

Steadily, with passion (♩ = 88)

Fare - well, my Li - la. I'll write ev - 'ry

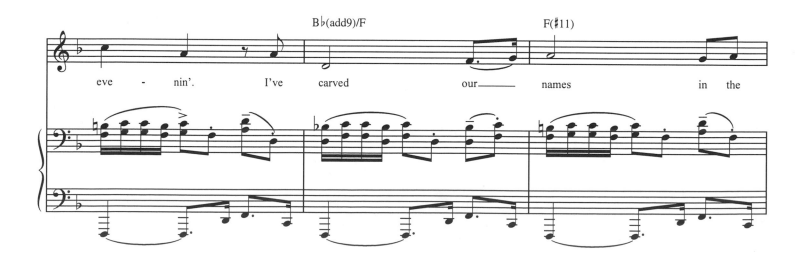

eve - nin'. I've carved our____ names in the

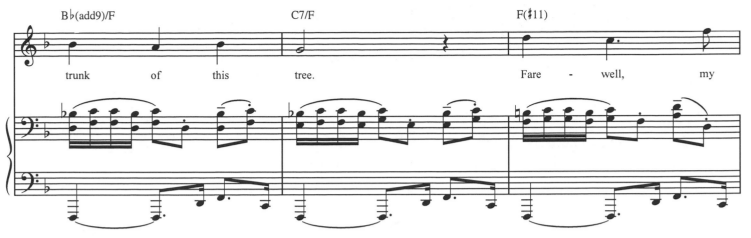

trunk of this tree. Fare - well, my

Li - la. I miss you al - read-y,_____ and

dream of the day when I'll hold you a -

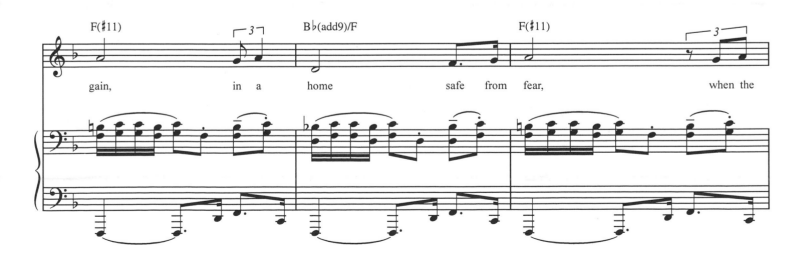

gain, in a home safe from fear, when the

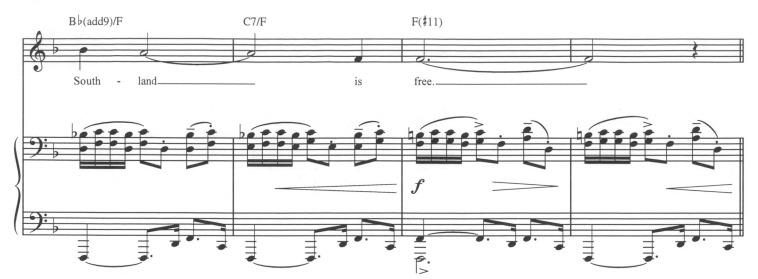

South - land_____ is free._____

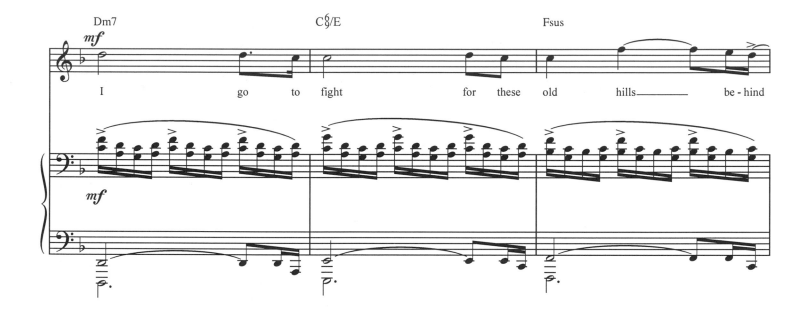

I   go   to fight   for these old   hills_____ be - hind

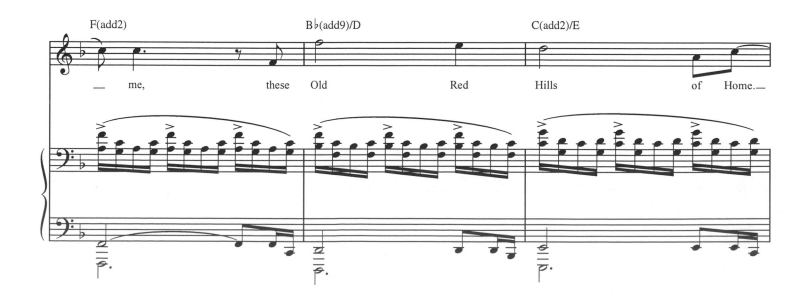

____ me,   these Old   Red   Hills   of Home._

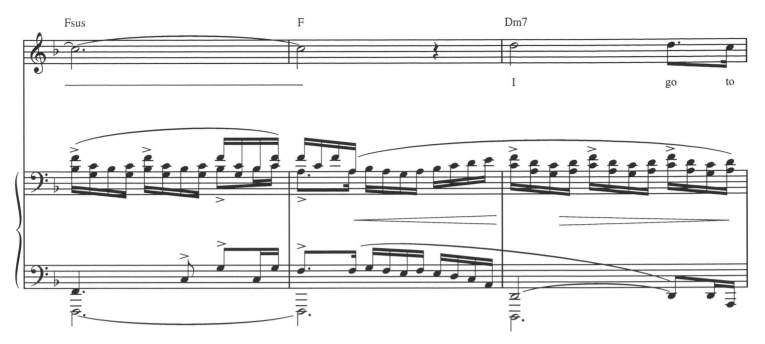

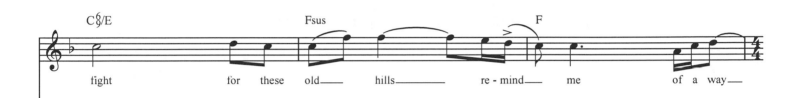

that must en - dure, in a town

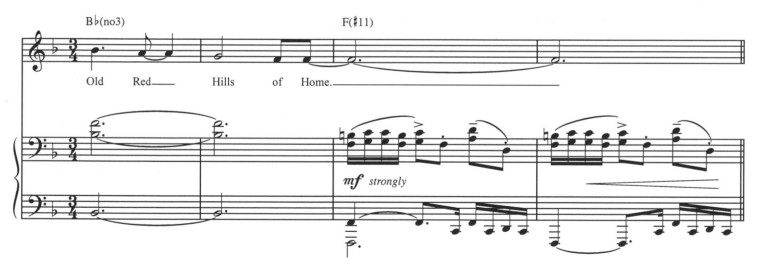

called Ma - ri - et - ta, in the

Old Red Hills of Home.

Pray on this day! As I jour - ney be - yond

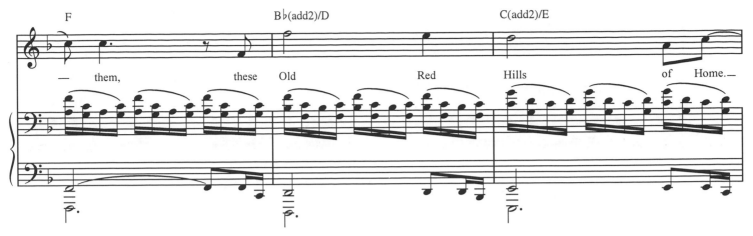

them, these Old Red Hills of Home.

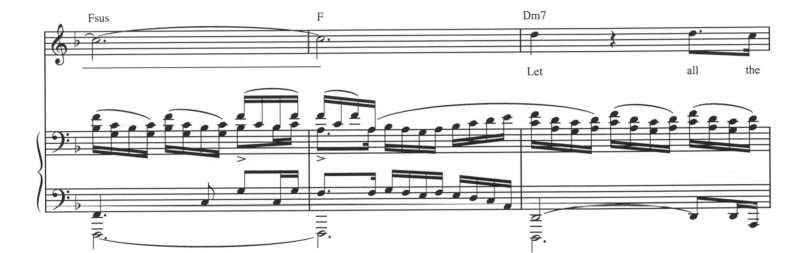

Let all the

blood of the North spill up-on them, 'til they've

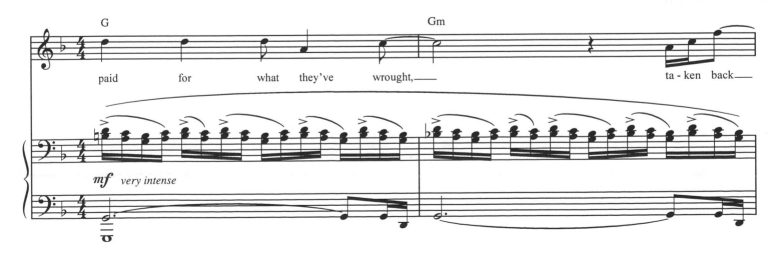

paid for what they've wrought, ta-ken back

the lies____ they've taught,____ and there's

peace in_____ Ma - ri - et - ta, and we're

safe a - gain____ in Geor - gia, in the land____

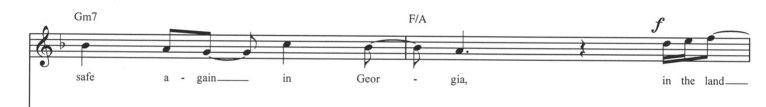

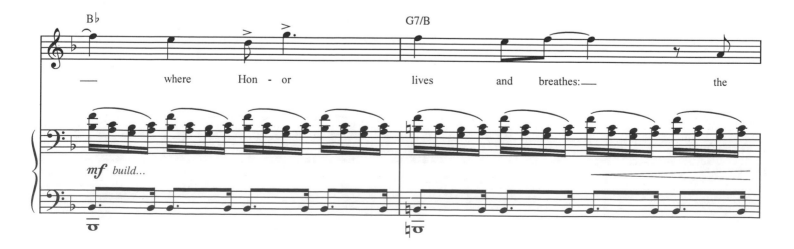

____ where Hon - or lives and breathes:____ the

THIS IS NOT OVER YET

from *Parade*

Music and Lyrics by
JASON ROBERT BROWN

* *This is a duet in the show.*

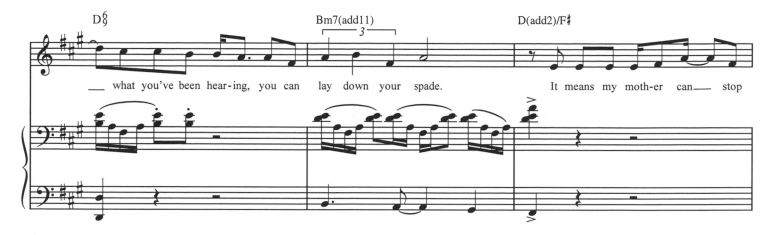

what you've been hear-ing, you can lay down your spade. It means my moth-er can stop

cry - ing. My rab - bi's eu - lo - gy can wait.

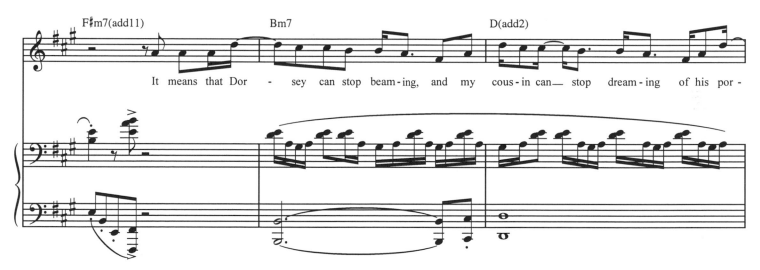

It means that Dor - sey can stop beam-ing, and my cous-in can stop dream-ing of his por -

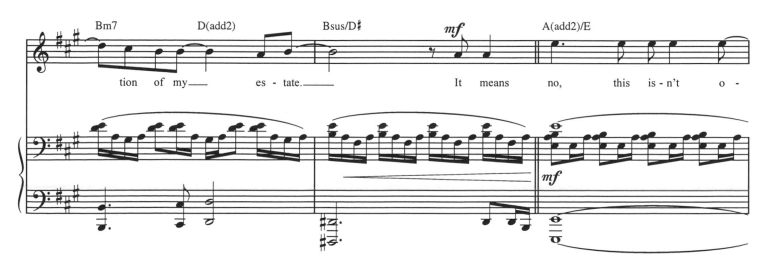

tion of my es - tate. It means no, this is - n't o -

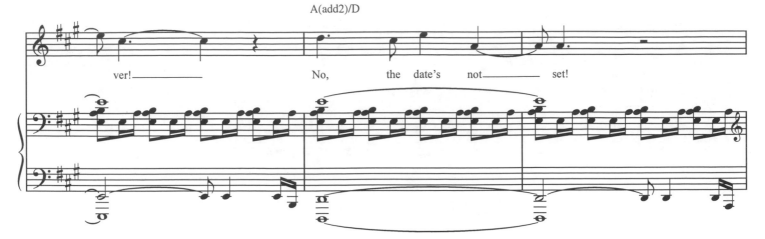

A(add2)/D

ver!_____ No, the date's not_____ set!

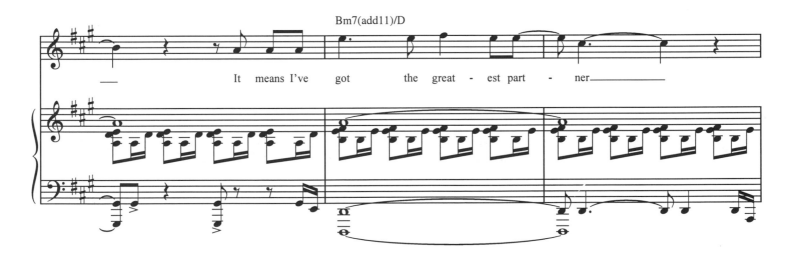

F#m9

No, I won't wake up to-mor-row, drown - ing in___ my___ sweat!___

Asus/G#

Bm7(add11)/D

___ It means I've got the great - est part - ner_____

A(add2)/C#

an - y man___ can get!___ It means I'll nev - er, ev - er, ev - er un-der-

mp

Bm7#13

es - ti - mate that wom - an 'cause this is not o - ver_____

Amaj7

__ yet!

Asus2

mp

Tell my un - cle not to wor - ry! Tell the reap - er not to

F#m7(add11)

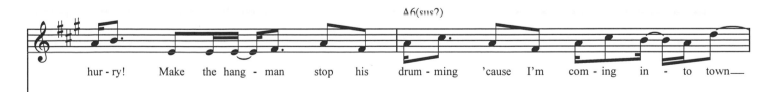

A6(sus2)

hur - ry! Make the hang - man stop his drum - ming 'cause I'm com - ing in - to town__

to win___ the day! Some-how I have-n't, with my schem-ing, screwed things

up be-yond___ re-deem-ing, and we're fi-nal-ly on___ our way!___

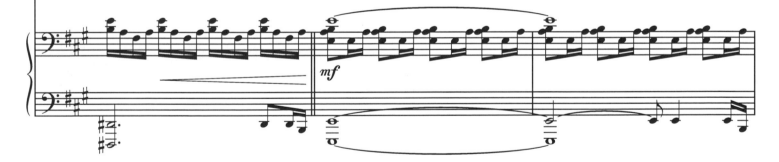

___ And no, this is-n't o-ver!___

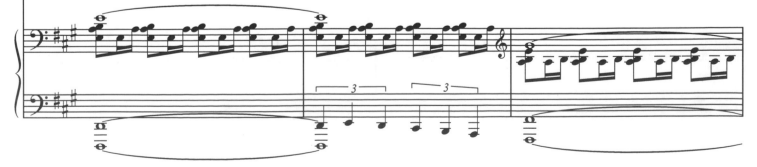

Hell, it's just be-gun!___ Hail the res-ur-rec-

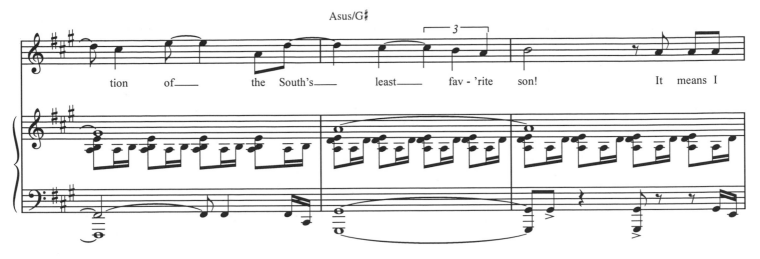

tion of—— the South's—— least—— fav-'rite son! It means I

made a vow—— for bet-ter!———— Two is bet-ter than

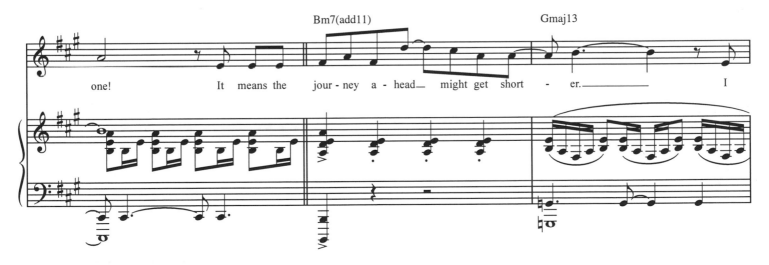

one! It means the jour-ney a-head—— might get short - er.———— I

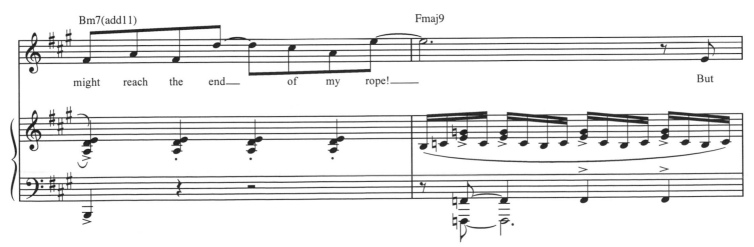

might reach the end—— of my rope!—— But

sud - den - ly, loud___ as a mor - tar,___ there is

hope!___ Fi - nal - ly,

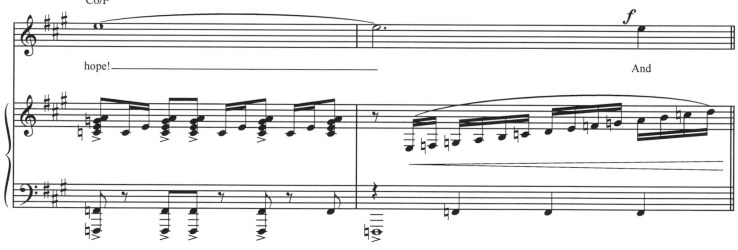

hope!___ And

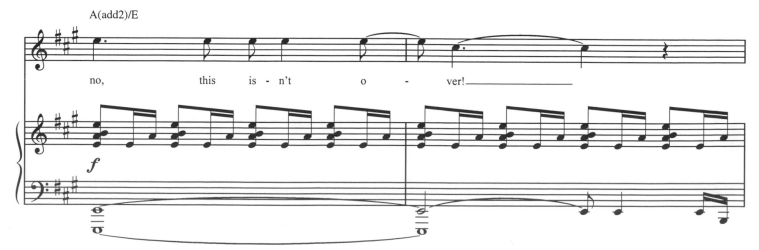

no, this is - n't o - ver!___

A(add2)/C#

things I see in you! It means a

Bm7(add11)

man who is-n't guilt-y does-n't have to walk the plank! It means the

gal-lows still are va-cant, and we've got my wife to thank! It means you

should-n't un-der-es-ti-mate Lu-cille and Le-o

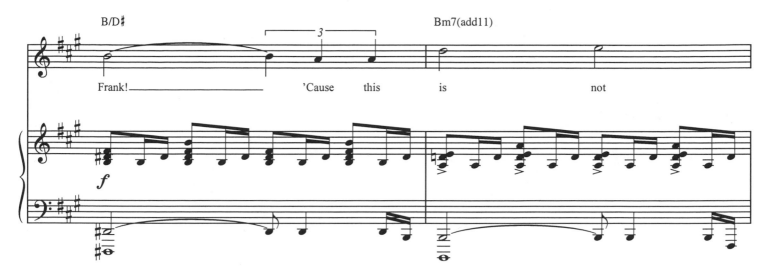

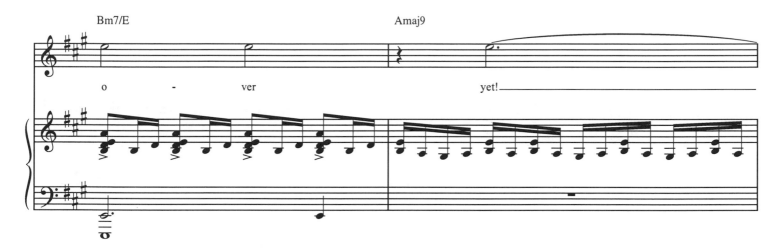

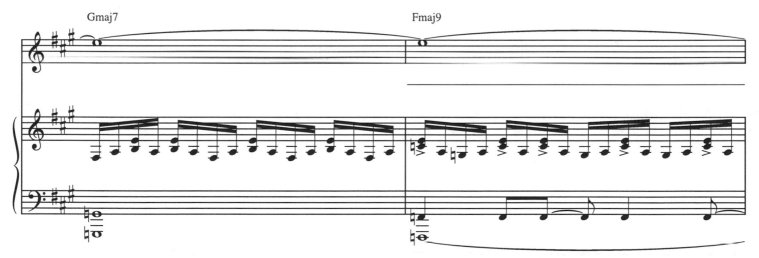

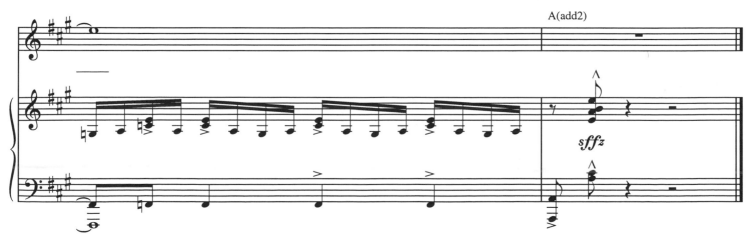

CORNER OF THE SKY

from *Pippin*

Words and Music by
STEPHEN SCHWARTZ

Moderately fast

Pippin:

Ev-'ry-thing has its sea - son, _____ ev-'ry-thing has its time. _

Show me a rea - son and _ I'll soon _ show you _ a _ rhyme. _

Cats sit on the win - dow-sill, ____ chil - dren sit in the show. _

Why do I feel I __ don't fit __ in an - y - where __ I go? _____

Riv - ers be - long __ where they __ can ram - ble;

ea - gles be - long __ where they __ can fly. __

I've got to be __ where my spir - it can run free, __

Thun-der clouds __ have their_ light-ning. ___ Night-in-gales have_ their song _____ and _

__ don't you see I want_ my life _ to be some-thing more_than long. _

Riv - ers be - long_ where they can ram - ble; ____

ea - gles be - long where they _ can fly. ___

I've got to be __ where my spir-it can __ run free, __

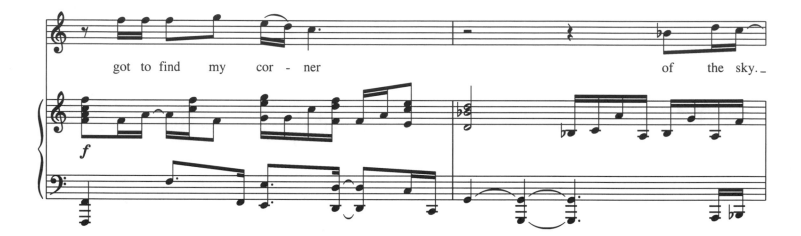

got to find my cor - ner of the sky. __

So man-y men __ seem des-tined _____ to set-tle for some - thing small,

but I __ won't rest un - til __ I know __ I have it all. _____ So

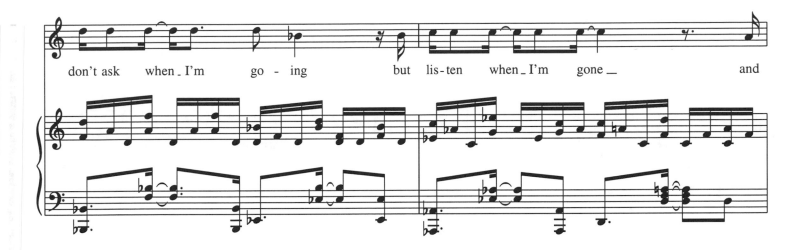

don't ask when __ I'm go - ing but lis - ten when __ I'm gone __ and

far a - way __ you'll hear me sing-ing soft - ly to the dawn. __

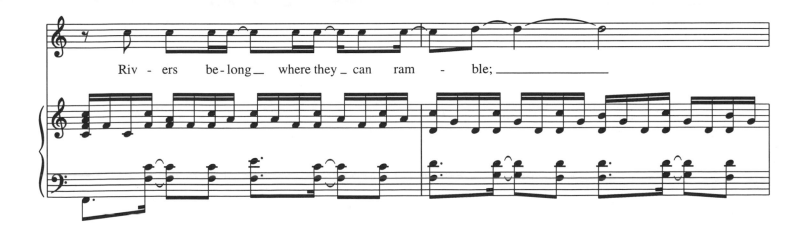

Riv - ers be - long __ where they __ can ram - ble; _____

ea - gles be-long where they __ can fly. __

I've got to be __ where my spir-it can __ run free, __

got to find my cor - ner __

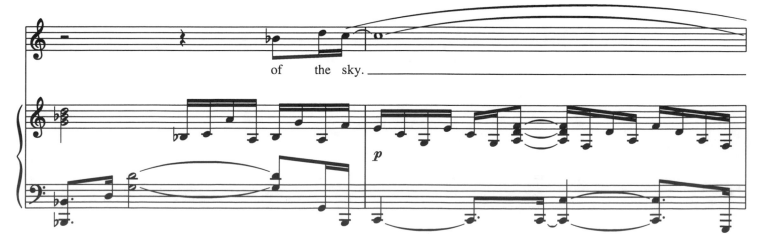

of the sky. __

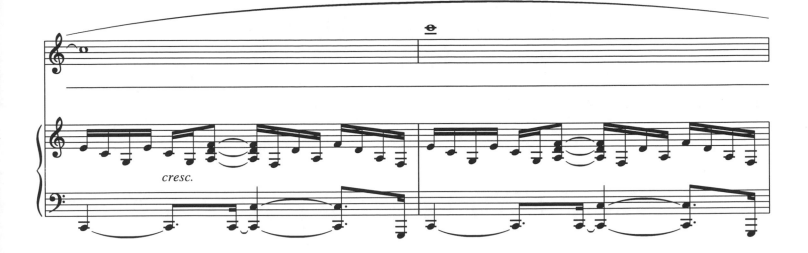

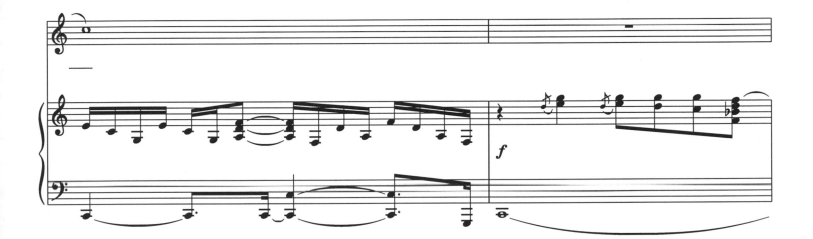

OH, IS THERE NOT ONE MAIDEN BREAST

from *The Pirates of Penzance*

Words by W.S. GILBERT
Music by ARTHUR SULLIVAN

will - ing - ly   All   mat - ri - mo - nial   am - bi - tion,   To

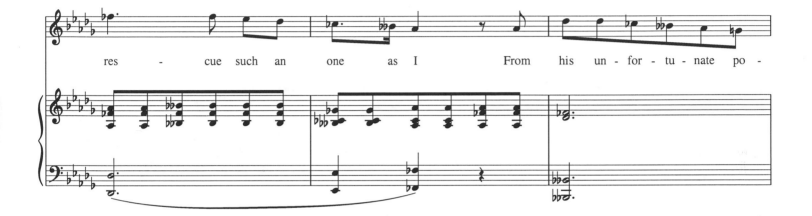

res - cue   such   an   one   as   I   From   his   un - for - tu - nate   po -

si - tion,   From   his ____ po - si - tion,   To   res   cue   such   an

one   as   I   From   his ____ un - for - tu - nate   po - si -

FREDERIC:

tion?   Oh,

is   there not one maid-en here   Whose home-ly face and bad com-plex - ion   Have

caused   all hope to dis-ap-pear   Of ev - er win-ning man's af - fec - tion?   To

such   an one,   If   such   there be,   I swear, by heav-en's arch a - bove   you,   If

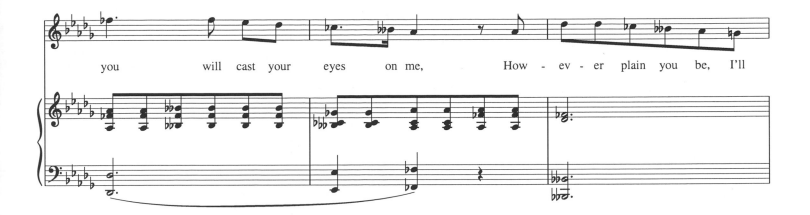

you will cast your eyes on me, How - ev - er plain you be, I'll

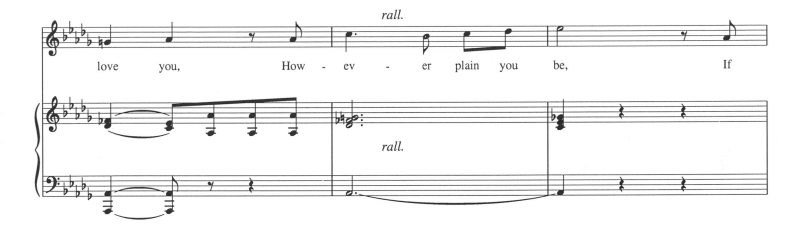

love you, How - ev - er plain you be, If

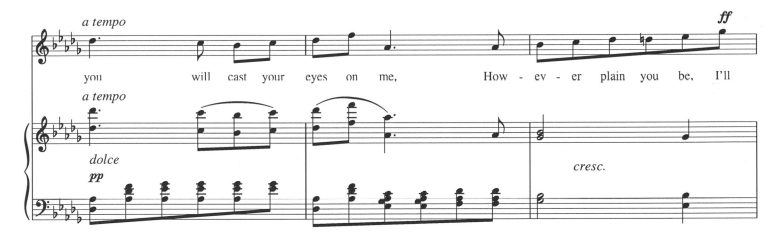

you will cast your eyes on me, How - ev - er plain you be, I'll

love _____ you, I'll love _____ you, I'll love, _____ I'll love ____ you!

ONE SONG GLORY

from *Rent*

Words and Music by
JONATHAN LARSON

go. Glo - ry, one song to leave be - hind.___

___ Find one song, one last re - frain._

___ Glo - ry ___ from the pret - ty boy front man ___

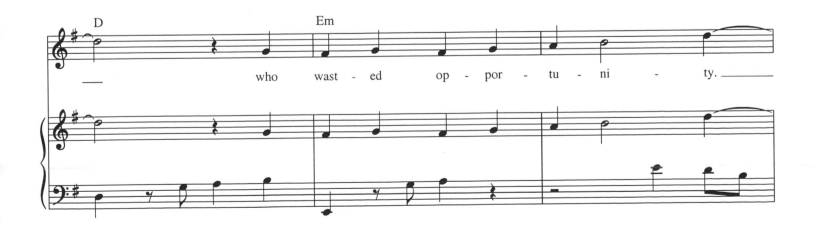

___ who wast - ed op - por - tu - ni - ty. ___

One song,___ he had the world at his feet. Glo - ry___

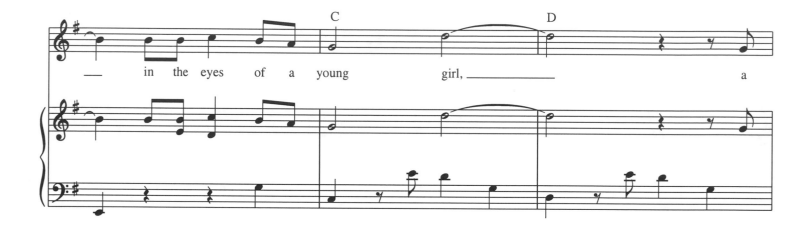

___ in the eyes of a young girl,_____ a

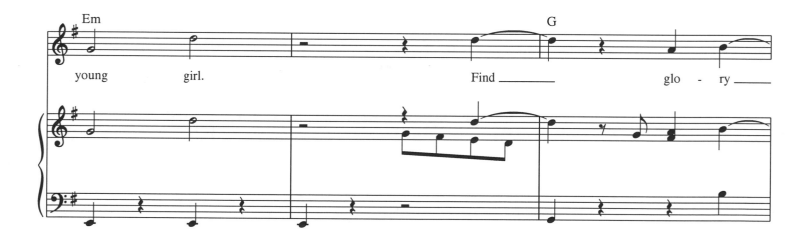

young girl. Find_____ glo - ry_____

___ be - yond the cheap col - ored lights, one song___ be - fore the sun sets.

Glo - ry on an - oth - er emp -

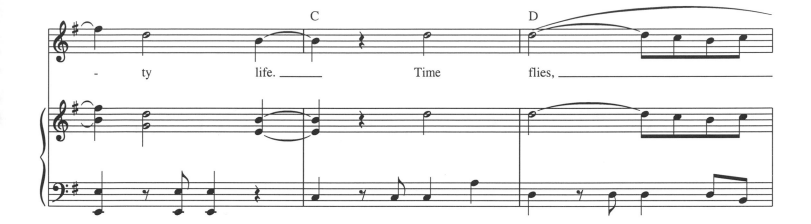

- ty life. _____ Time flies, _____

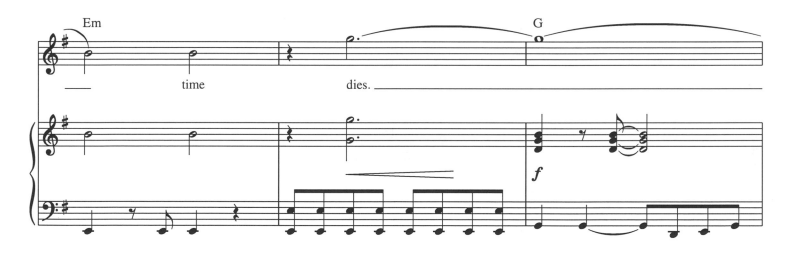

_____ time dies. _____

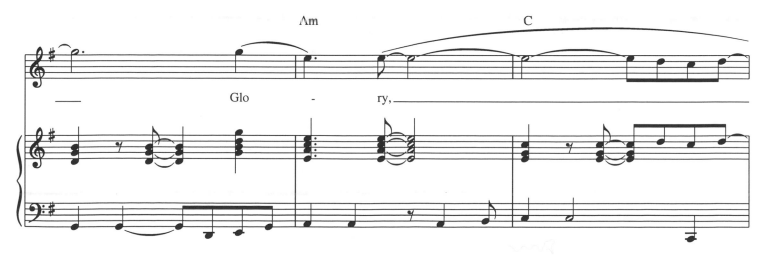

_____ Glo - ry, _____

one blaze of glo -

- ry. _____ One blaze of

glo - ry. _____

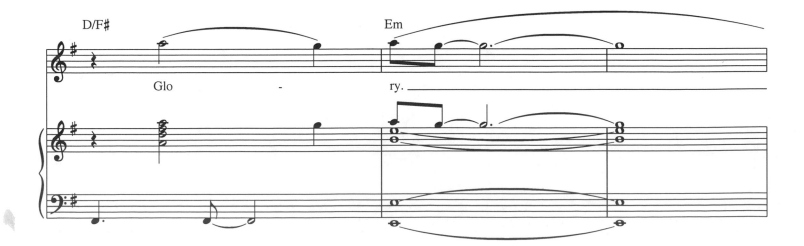

Glo - ry. _____

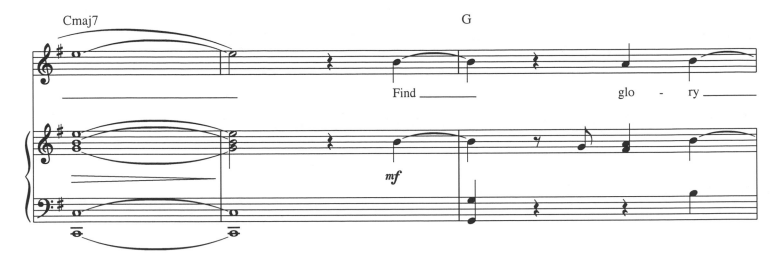

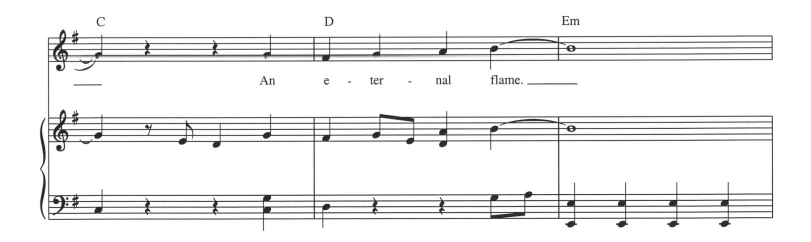

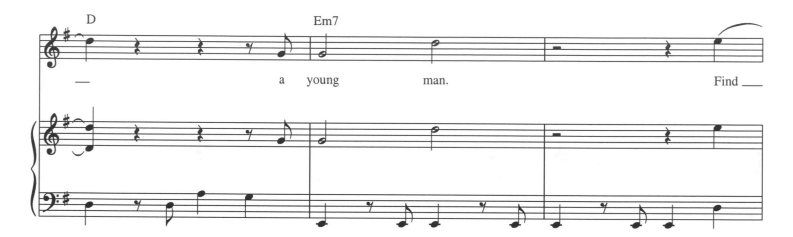

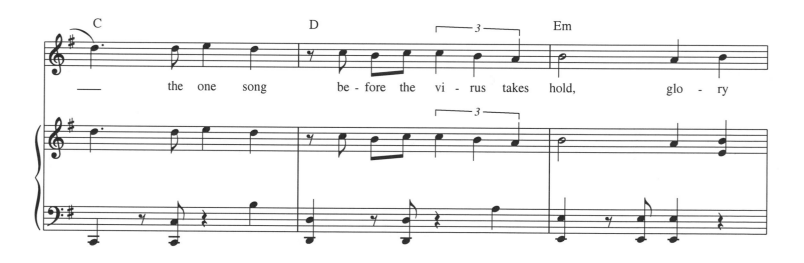

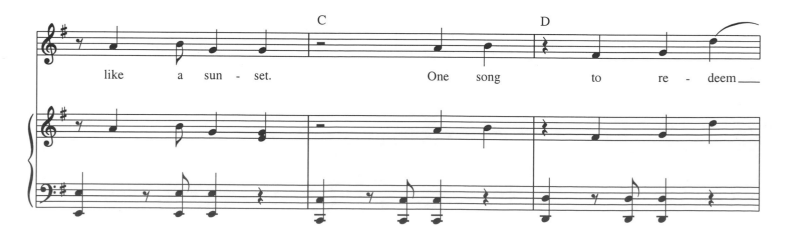

YOUR EYES

from *Rent*

Words and Music by
JONATHAN LARSON

Moderately

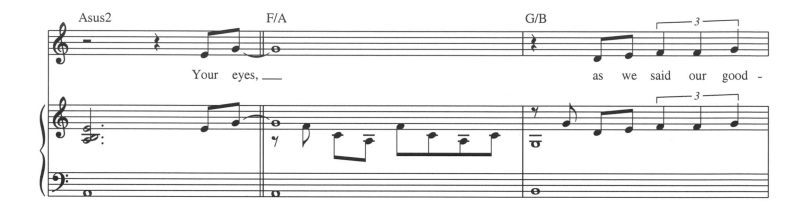

Your eyes, ___ as we said our good-

byes, can't get them out of my mind. And I

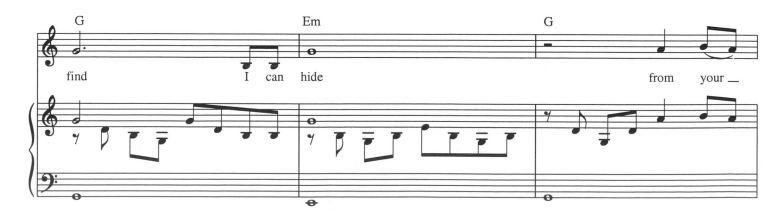

find I can hide from your ___

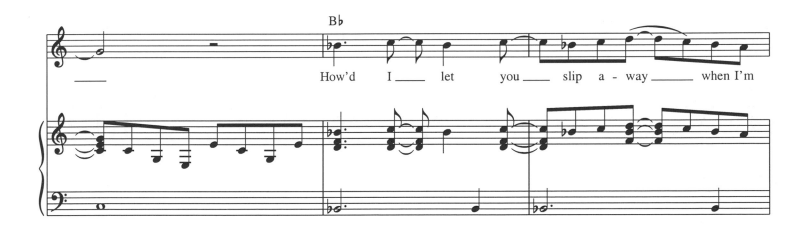

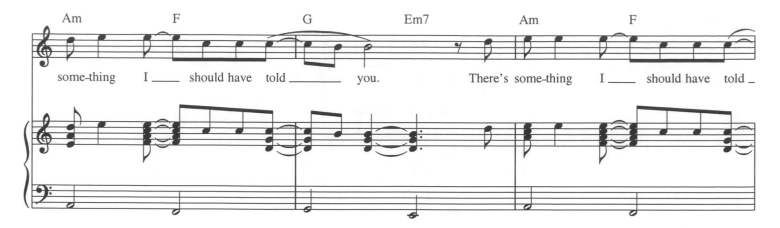

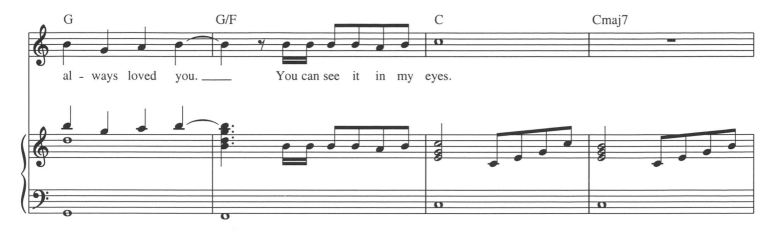

al - ways loved you. _____ You can see it in my eyes.

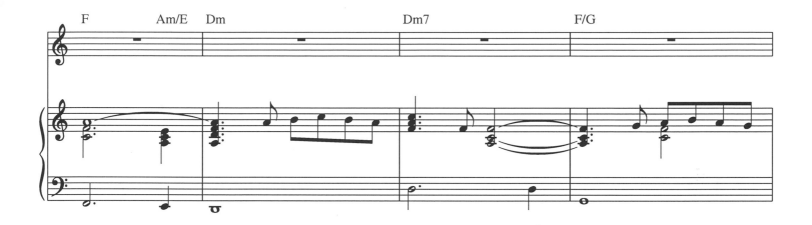

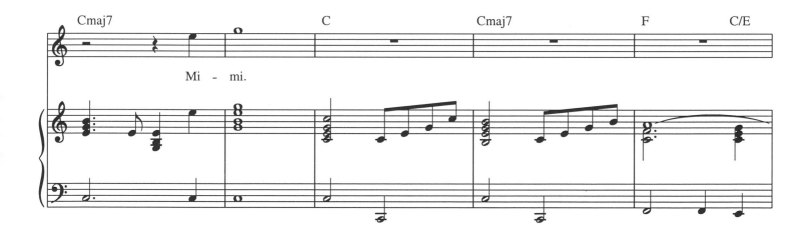

Mi - mi.

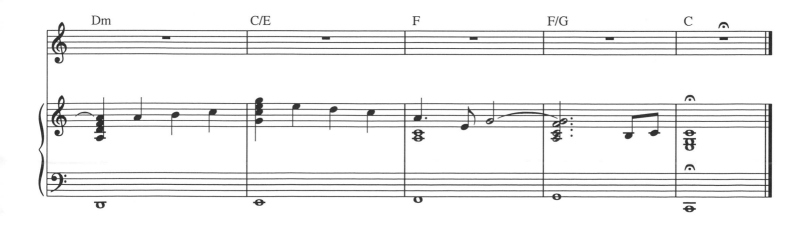

SUNSET BOULEVARD
from *Sunset Boulevard*

Music by ANDREW LLOYD WEBBER
Lyrics by DON BLACK and CHRISTOPHER HAMPTON,
with contributions by AMY POWERS

JOE

Sure, I came out here to make my name, want-ed my pool, my dose of

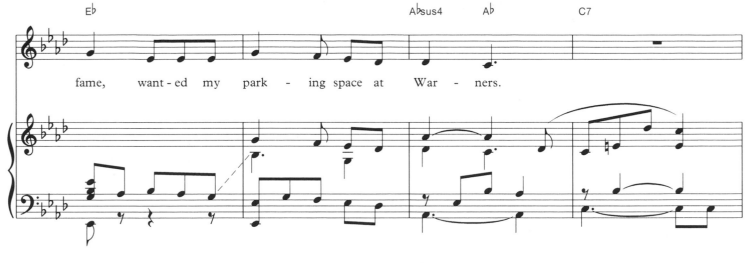

Eb ... **Absus4** **Ab** ... **C7**

fame, want-ed my park - ing space at War - ners.

Fm ... **Db**

But af - ter a year, a one room hell, a mur-phy bed, a ran-cid

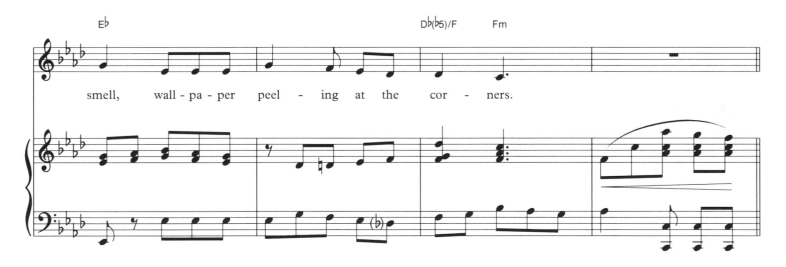

Eb ... **Db(b5)/F** **Fm**

smell, wall-pa-per peel - ing at the cor - ners.

Eb ... **Bb/D**

Sun - set Bou - le-vard, twist - ing bou - le-vard, se - cre-tive and

rich, a lit - tle sca - ry. Sun - set Bou - le-vard,

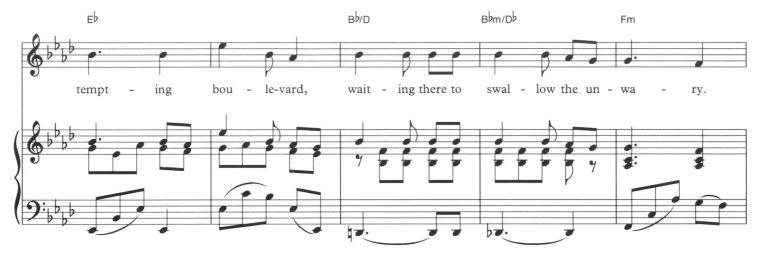

tempt - ing bou - le-vard, wait - ing there to swal - low the un - wa - ry.

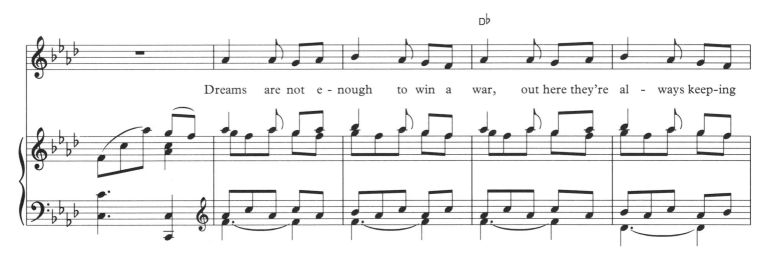

Dreams are not e - nough to win a war, out here they're al - ways keep-ing

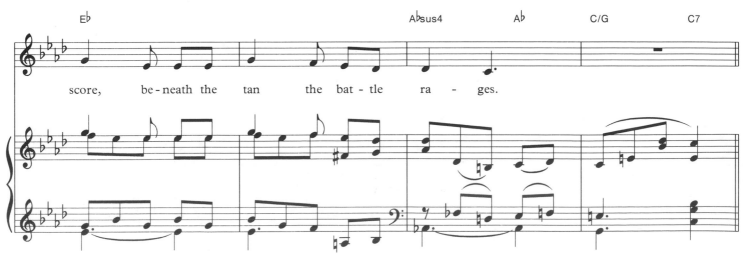

score, be - neath the tan the bat - tle ra - ges.

Smile a rent-ed smile, fill some-one's glass, kiss some-one's wife, kiss some-one's

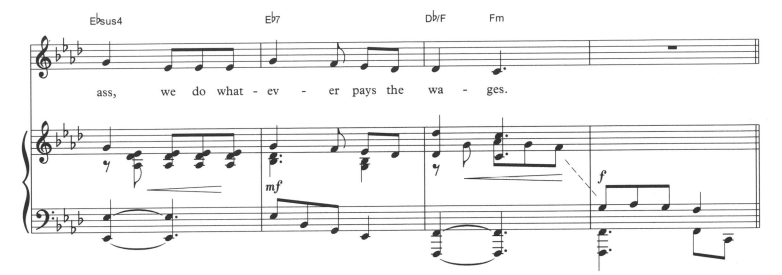

ass, we do what-ev - er pays the wa - ges.

Sun - set Bou - le - vard, head - line bou - le - vard,

get - ting here is on - ly the be - gin - ning.

Sun - set Bou - le - vard, jack - pot bou - le - vard,

once you've won you have to go on win - ning.

You think I've sold out? Dead right, I've sold out, I've just been wait - ing

for the right of - fer, comf - 'ta - ble quart-ers, re - gu - lar ra - tions, twen - ty - four hour

five star room ser - vice. And if I'm ho - nest I like the la - dy.

I can't help be - ing touched by her fol - ly. I'm tread - ing wa - ter,

tak - ing the mo - ney, watch - ing her sun - set. Well, I'm a wri - ter.

L. A.'s changed a lot ov - er the years since those brave

gold - rush pi - on - eers came in their crea - ky co-vered wa - gons.

Far as they could go, end of the line, their dreams were yours, their dreams were

mine, but in those dreams were hid - den dra - gons.

Sun - set Bou - le - vard, fren - zied bou - le - vard,

swamped with ev - 'ry kind of false e - mo - tion.

Sun - set Bou - le - vard, bru - tal bou - le - vard,

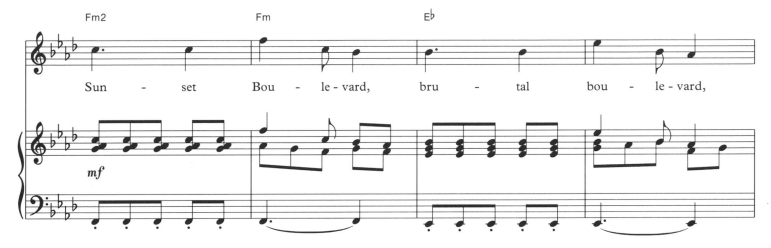

just like you we'll wind up in the o - cean.

She was sink - ing fast, I threw a rope, now I have suits and she has

hope, it seemed an e - le - gant so - lu - tion.

One day this must end, it is - n't real, still I'll en - joy a hear - ty

meal be - fore to - mor - row's ex - e - cu - tion.

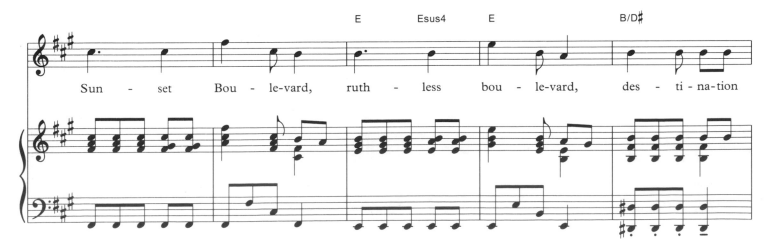

Sun - set Bou - le - vard, ruth - less bou - le - vard, des - ti - na - tion

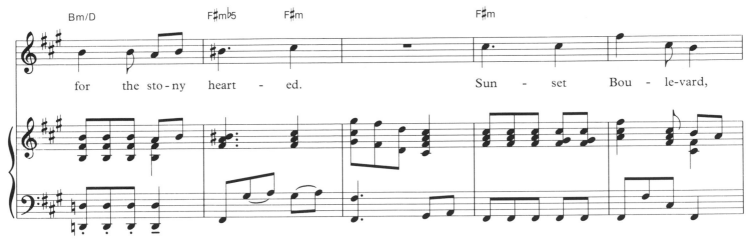

for the sto-ny heart - ed. Sun - set Bou - le-vard,

le - thal bou - le-vard, ev - 'ry-one's for - got - ten how they

start - ed here on Sun - set Bou - le - vard.____

ISN'T THIS A LOVELY DAY
(To Be Caught in the Rain?)
from the RKO Radio Motion Picture *Top Hat*

Words and Music by
IRVING BERLIN

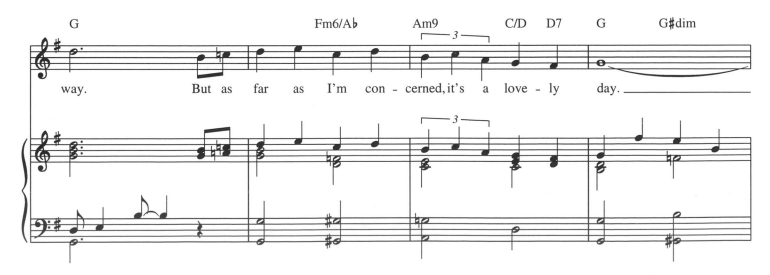

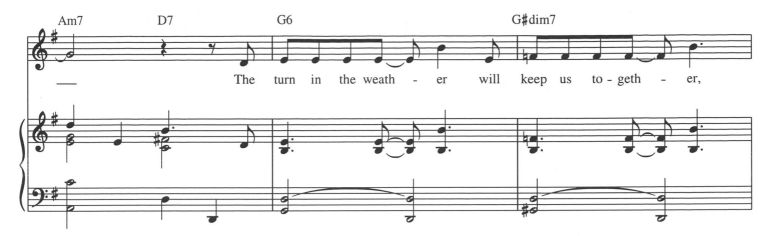

The turn in the weath - er will keep us to - geth - er,

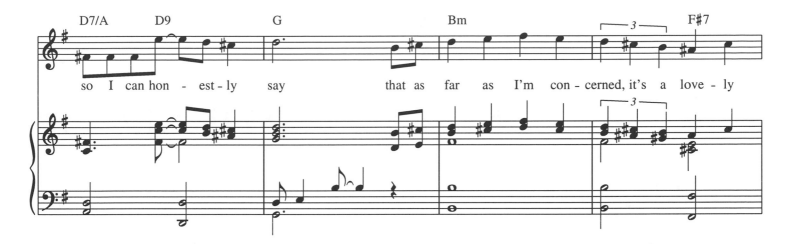

so I can hon - est - ly say that as far as I'm con - cerned, it's a love - ly

day _____ and ev - 'ry - thing's O. K. _____

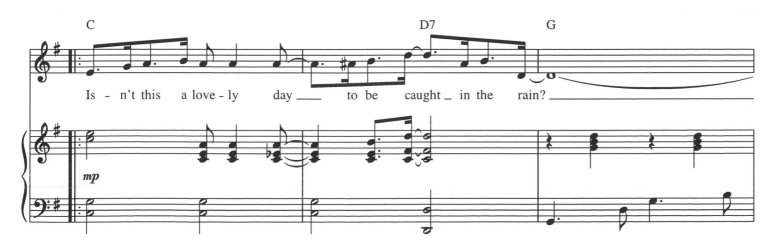

Is - n't this a love - ly day ___ to be caught _ in the rain? _____

You were go - ing on your way, __ now you've got __ to re - main. __

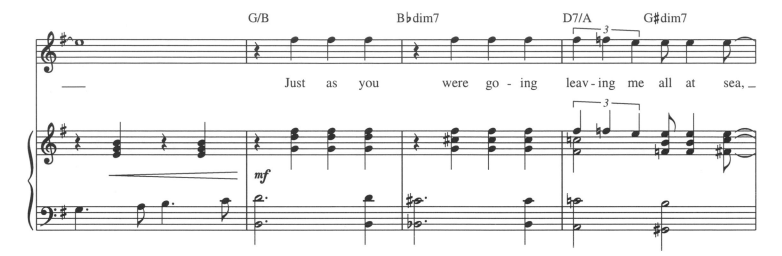

Just as you were go - ing leav - ing me all at sea, __ the clouds broke.

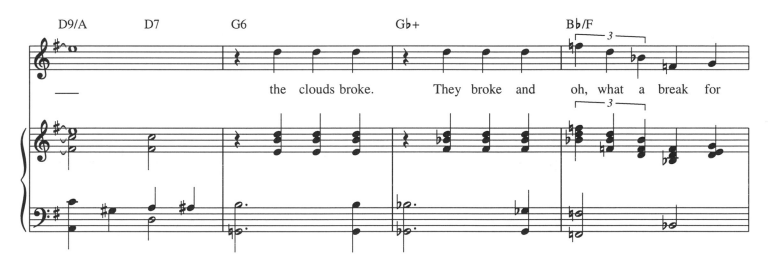

They broke and oh, what a break for me.

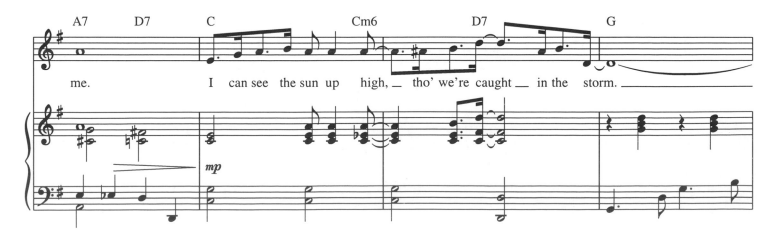

I can see the sun up high, __ tho' we're caught __ in the storm. __

I can see where you and I ___ could be co - zy and warm. ___

___ Let the rain pit - ter pat - ter but it real - ly does- n't mat - ter if the

skies are gray. ___ Long as I can be with you, ___ it's a love - ly

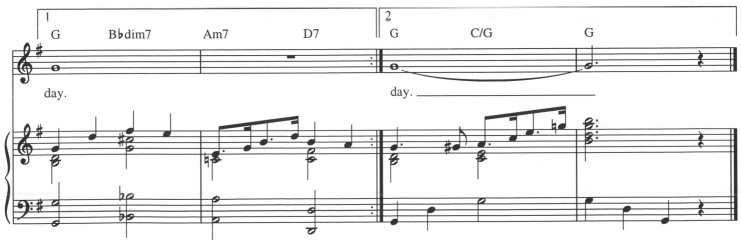

day. day. ___

QUASIMODO
from Howard Crabtree's *When Pigs Fly*

Music by DICK GALLAGHER
Lyrics by MARK WALDROP

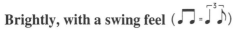

Brightly, with a swing feel

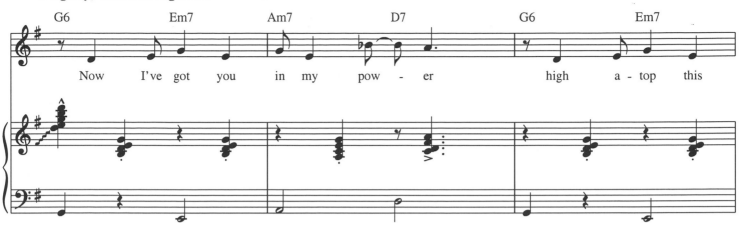

Now I've got you in my pow - er high a - top this

Goth - ic tow - er. There's death be - low and heav - en a -

bove! _____ While the gates of

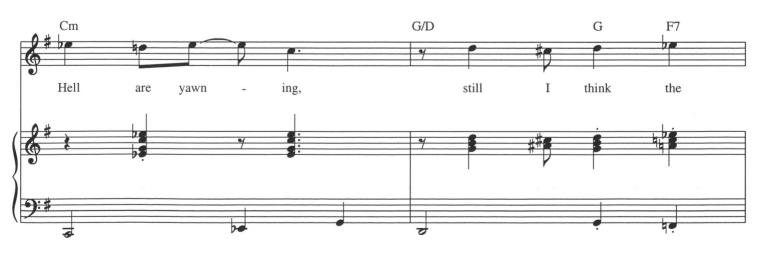

Hell are yawn - ing, still I think the

truth is dawn - ing: I've got a hunch _ I'm in love! _

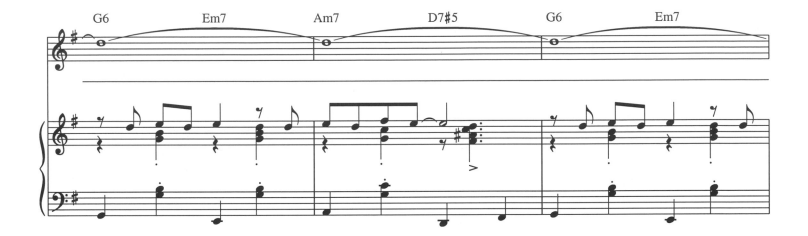

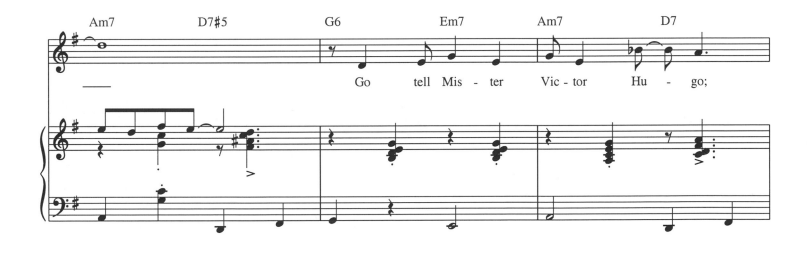

_ Go tell Mis - ter Vic - tor Hu - go;

kid, where I go, that's where you _ go!

We're fly - ing on the wings _ of a dove! _____

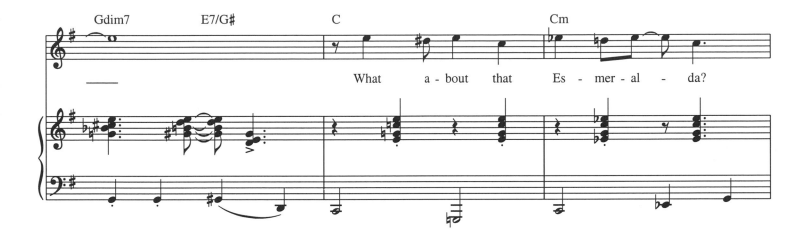

_____ What a - bout that Es - mer - al - da?

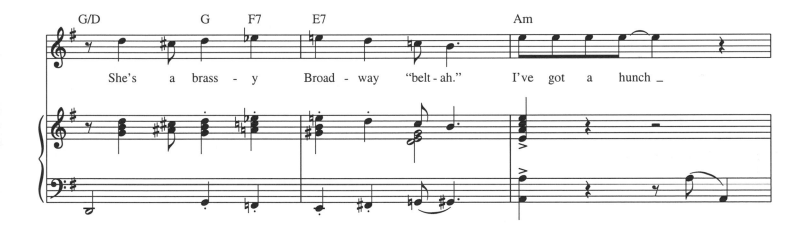

She's a brass - y Broad - way "belt - ah." I've got a hunch _

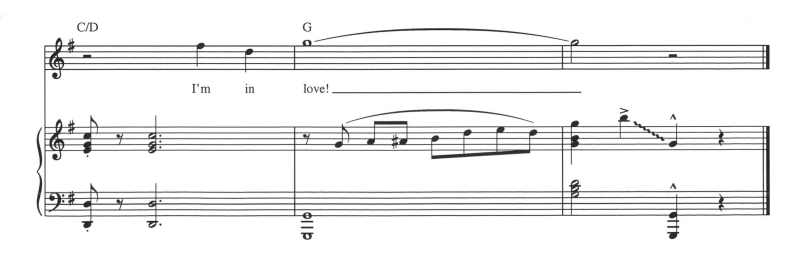

I'm in love! _____

THE MASON
from the Broadway musical *Working*

Music and Lyric by
CRAIG CARNELIA

197

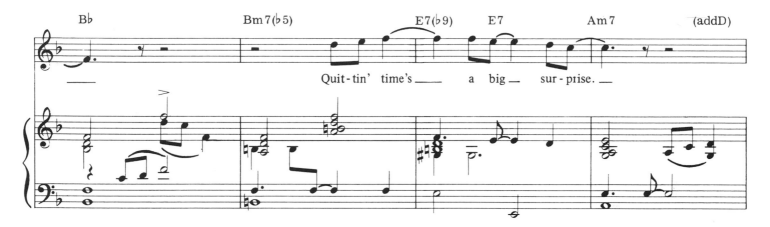

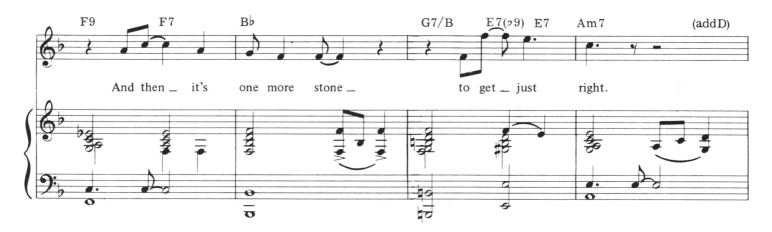

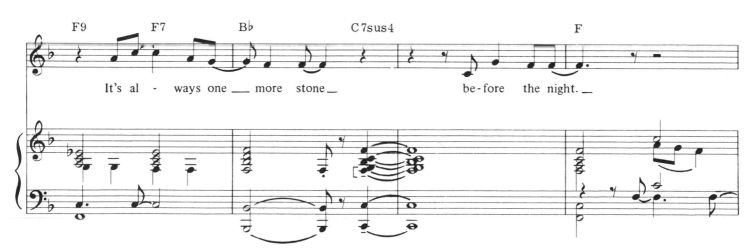

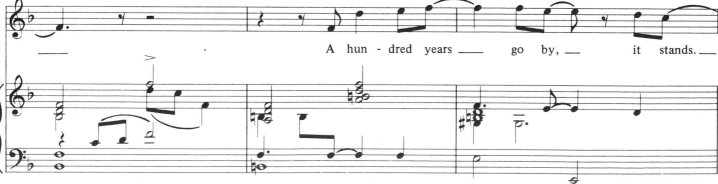

COFFEE (IN A CARDBOARD CUP)

from *70, Girls, 70*

Words and Music by FRED EBB
and JOHN KANDER

Brightly

THE PROPOSAL
from *Titanic*

Music and Lyrics
MAURY YESTON

In the show this number moves into a duet with the telegraph operator; it has been adapted as a solo here.

May God's heav-en be your blan-ket as you soft-ly sleep.

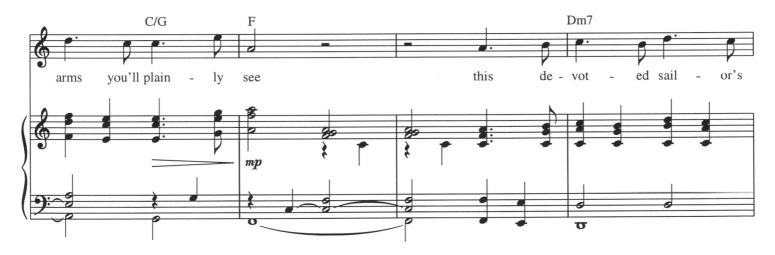

Mar - ry me! _____ When you're fi - n'lly in my

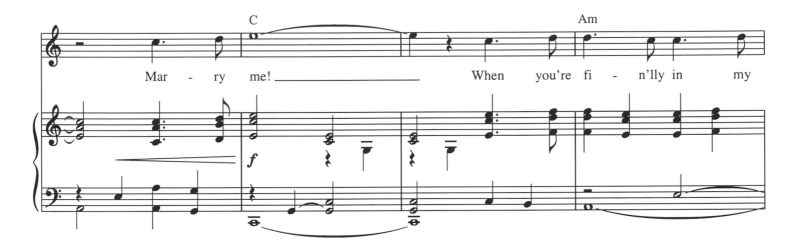

arms you'll plain - ly see this de - vot - ed sail - or's

heart and soul are yours to keep, _____

yours to keep... Mar - ry me! May the Lord ___

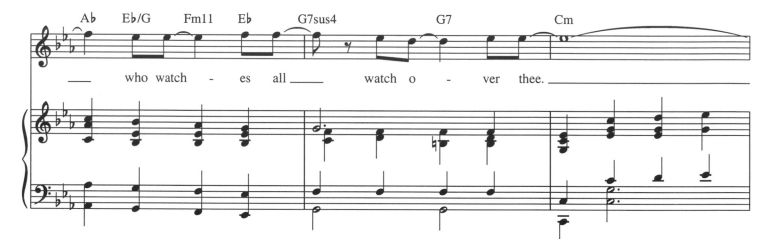

___ who watch - es all ___ watch o - ver thee. ___

___ Mar - ry

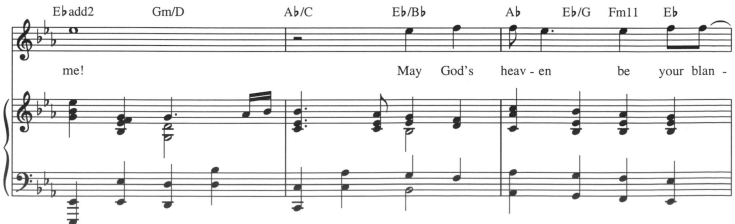

me! May God's heav - en be your blan -

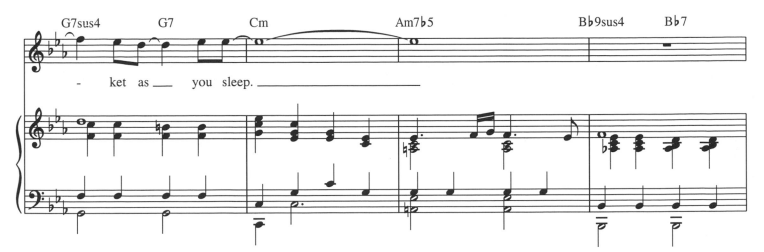

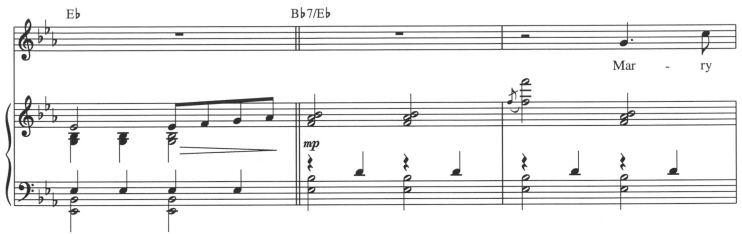

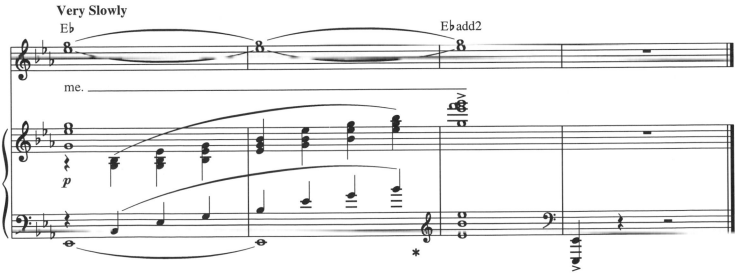

BARRETT'S SONG
from *Titanic*

Music and Lyrics by
MAURY YESTON

NO MOON
from *Titanic*

Music and Lyrics by
MAURY YESTON

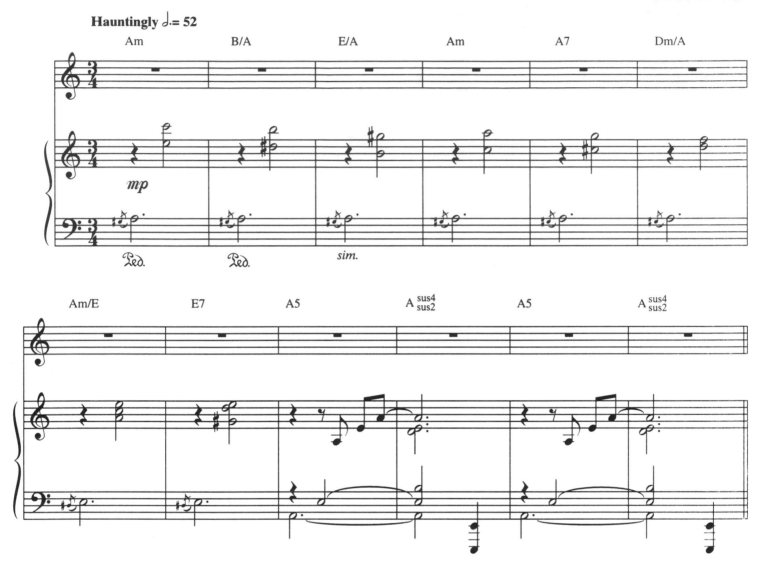

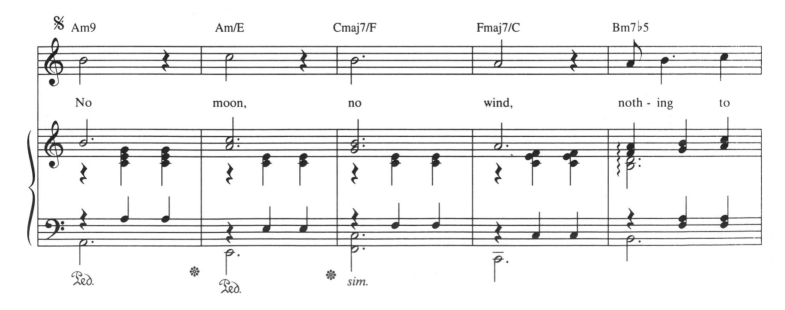

221

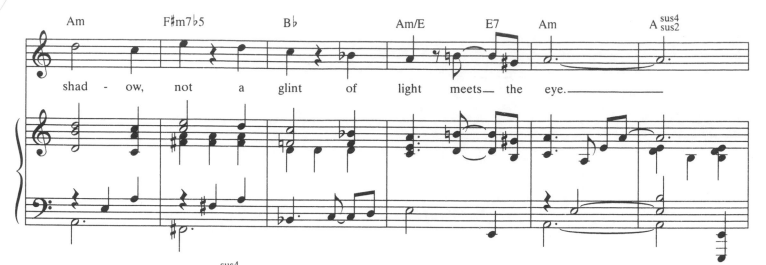

shad - ow, not a glint of light meets— the eye.

And we go sail - ing, sail -

ing ev - er west - ward on the sea. We go

sail - ing, sail - ing, ev - er

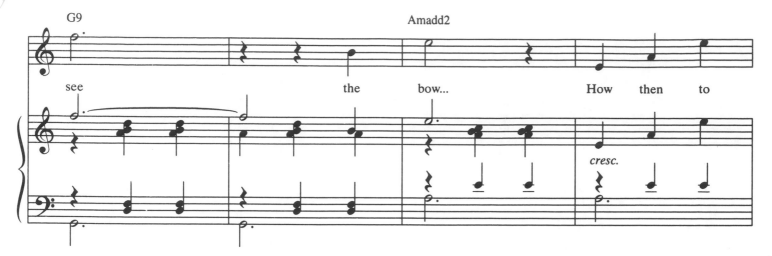

see ... the bow... How then to

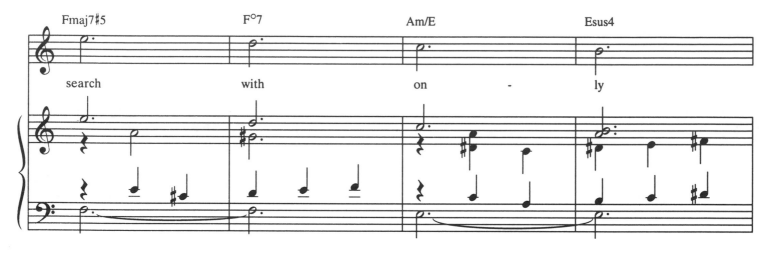

search with on - ly

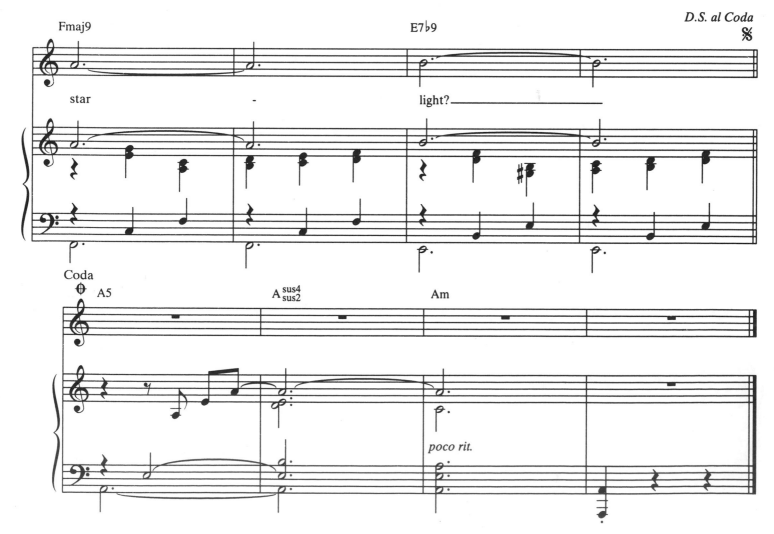

star - light? _____